THE BADMINTON COACH

This Book is Dedicated

to

CHARLES CUMPSTEY

A Good Friend and Partner

A Gifted Coach

and

A Very Gallant Fighter,

also to

His Wife, MARY, his Tower of Strength

THE
BADMINTON COACH

A Manual
for
Coaches, Teachers and Players

by

PAT DAVIS

National Coach of the Badminton Association of England,
Welsh International and Kent County Player

Approved by the English Schools' Badminton Association,
the Scottish Schools' Badminton Union
and the Scottish Badminton Union

KAYE & WARD
LONDON

First published by
Kaye & Ward Limited
21 New Street, London EC2M 4NT
1970
Reprinted with corrections and additions 1976

ISBN 0 7182 0837 4

Printed in Great Britain by
Fletcher & Son Ltd, Norwich

CONTENTS

Chapter		Page
	List of Illustrations	6
	Foreword	9
1.	The Qualities of a Coach	11
2.	Coaching Courses	14
3.	Putting a Lesson Across	17
4.	Coaching in Schools and Evening Institutes	26
5.	Equipment	41
6.	Basic Techniques	44
7.	Stroke Production and Correction	53
8.	Tactics	74
9.	Analysis of Strokes and Tactics	97
10.	Only *Perfect* Practice Makes Perfect	101
11.	Practices	107
12.	Conditioned Games	122
13.	Physical Fitness	126
14.	Mental Approach	141
15.	Coaching Advanced Players	150
16.	Value and Enjoyment of Coaching	159
	Acknowledgments	160

LIST OF ILLUSTRATIONS

Photographs

Between pages 32 *and* 33

1. The Author with four English internationals
GRIPS
2a. Forehand
2b. Backhand
3. Frying-pan
USE OF WRIST
4a. Cocked back
4b. In straight line with arm
5. Fully uncocked and brought over
SMASH
6. Taking up position
7. Backswing
8. Start of forward swing
9. Point of impact
JUMPING SMASH
10. Going up!
11. One point landing!
12. Tyna Barinaga smashing
ROUND-THE-HEAD SMASHES (Paul Whetnall)
13. Intercepting the shuttle
14. Just before impact

Between pages 64 *and* 65

MOVEMENT
15. Alertness – Margaret Allen
16. Paul Whetnall at full stretch
BACKHAND OVERHEAD CLEAR
17. Margaret Allen backswing
18. Just after impact
19. Follow-through
20. Pat Davis demonstrating
LOW SERVE
21. Just before impact – Peter Roper
22. Just after impact
23. Tyna Barinaga serving
BACKHAND SERVE
24. Beginning of forward swing – Ray Sharp
25. Fractionally after impact
DRIVES
26. Halfway through forward swing
27. Backhand at impact
28. After impact – Paul Whetnall
DEFENCE
29. Flat push return – the Author
30. Between the legs – Ray Sharp
31. Round the back – Ray Sharp

Between pages 96 *and* 97

NET SHOTS
32. Down – Margaret Allen
33. Upwards (forehand) –
   the Author
34. Upwards (backhand) –
   the Author
HIGH SERVE
35. Position of readiness
36. Just before impact
37. Point of impact
38. Follow-through
RETURN OF SERVE (Ray
Sharp)

39. Stance
40. Hitting down (Brush)
41. Hitting up
THE LOB (Backhand)
42. Moving in – Sue Whet-
   nall
43. Just before impact
44. Follow-through
45. Tyna Barinaga taking
   the shuttle
MEN'S DOUBLES
46. Basic opening positions
47. Attack and defence

Between pages 128 *and* 129

LADIES' DOUBLES
48. Margaret Allen and Sue
   Whetnall in action

MIXED
49. Half-court push attack
50. Interception and covering
51. Smash, interception and
   retrieve

COACHING
52. Shadowing

53. Twelve to a court
54. Warwick Shute demon-
   strating
55. Practice routines
56. Manual guidance –
   Peter Roper and Anne
   Smith
57. Twelve juniors on one
   court
58. Twenty-four to a court
59. Jumping smash – Pat
   Davis

Diagrams

Fig.   *Page*

1. Court test markings — 31
2. Class hitting against walls — 34
3. Clearing or dropping or smashing practice — 35
4. Practice routines — 36
5. Playing across width of hall — 37
6. Utilizing all floor space — 38
7. Court dimensions and nomenclature — 43
8. Movement backwards — 51
9. Movement cross-court — 51
10. Trajectories — 53
11. Trajectories of serves — 63
12. Correct and fault services — 64
13. Placements of return of smash — 71
14. Attack and defence positions — 76
15. Transition from attack to defence from clear — 77
16. Transition from attack to defence from lob — 78
17. Placements of doubles serves — 80
18. Returns of service in doubles — 81
19. Placements for attack from side of court — 83
20. Cross-courting — 87
21. Lady drops back to cover man when he rushes serve — 90
22. Attack against wedge defence — 91
23. Basic positions in singles — 92
24. Placements of singles serves — 93
25. Placements of returns of high serves (or clears) — 94
26. Sequence of shots in singles — 95
27. Simple push shots — 108
28. Throwing practices — 118
29. Rallying practices — 112
30. Complementary shots — 113
31. Rallying and footwork — 114
32. Running round game 1 — 115
33. Running round game 2 — 116
34. Clearing and footwork practice — 117
35. Elementary group practices — 118
36. Pattern driving — 120
37. Restricted singles — 124
38. Pressure training — 134
39. Agility exercises — 136
40. Advanced consistency exercises — 152

FOREWORD

We are conscious of the great honour accorded to us by the author, Pat Davis, in inviting us to write the Foreword of his second book, *The Badminton Coach*. His first, *Badminton Complete*, which fulfilled its title without doubt, was acclaimed by all who read it.

The Badminton Coach is more advanced and provides a very comprehensive study of the techniques and tactics of the game; moreover, it is well illustrated.

As teachers, we feel it provides a very helpful guide to lesson planning and gives numerous suggestions for dealing with difficult situations i.e. large classes and one court, etc. Every aspect of coaching has been dealt with in great detail, including the psychological angle, which is so important if coaching sessions are going to be successful. It is also an ideal manual for teachers, coaches, P.E. Organizers, Club leaders and players. They cannot fail to find it an essential work of reference.

Pat, a former Welsh International, ultimately turned to coaching, where he found instant success, having the natural ability to pass on his vast experience gained during his playing career. Thousands of eager and enthusiastic players will benefit considerably from the instructions and information given in detail in this book, as well as coaches and aspiring coaches.

Coaching demands much careful thought, hard work and discipline on the part of the coach, but there is nothing more satisfying than helping other players, whether young or old, not only to improve, but to enjoy this fascinating game.

Although England has achieved a number of successes in top class play, we still have a long way to go to compete with the great strength and depth in play of such countries as Indonesia, Malaysia and Denmark. It is only by 'spreading the Gospel',

9

through players and particularly Coaches, that we shall improve our overall standard.

So go to it Coaches and would-be Coaches, read this book and get cracking!

Margaret Allen

Susan Whetnall

Kent and England.
All-England Ladies' Doubles
Champions, 1969 and 1970.
Gold Medal winners,
Commonwealth Games 1970.

Symbols Used in Diagrams

———2———→		Shuttle's line of flight
- - - - 1 - - -→		Players' movements
o 1st ... Subsequent }		Players' positions
▥		Target area
|		Point of impact
A	Attacker	D Defender
L	Lady	M Man
S	Server	R Receiver
Fe	Feeder	Fa Fag
	SP Server's partner	

I

THE QUALITIES OF A COACH

Many a badminton enthusiast has been deterred from becoming a coach because he thought that, almost overnight, miraculously, he had to become a paragon of all the virtues. Admittedly, the coach must stand out from his students at whatever level he is coaching, but the qualities he needs can all be achieved with thought, practice and effort.

TURN OUT
Every coach should be beyond reproach in his smartness on court. Filthy shoes are not the hallmark of a great player but rather that of a sloven. White shorts, shirt, socks and sweater should be immaculate. A track-suit (with BA of E badge), not old grey flannels, gives necessary warmth in a cold hall. Such smartness engenders self-confidence and class confidence (Plate 1).

VOICE
Effective voice production is essential to hold a class.
    Breath control is its basis. The coach should stand erect but relaxed before his class, filling his lungs through the nose by drawing his ribs upwards and outwards; controlled retention and release is more important than sheer quantity (cf a sponge). Only by full and active use of lower jaw, tongue, lips and clear nasal passages will he articulate clearly and resonantly. This is particularly important with consonants : the explosives, fricatives and nasal sounds. He must open his mouth so that he does not speak through clenched teeth. The end of a sentence should be as clear and unhurried as the beginning.
    The coach should stand far enough away from the class to force himself, not to shout, but at least to project his voice to the student farthest from him. He should wait for complete

11

silence before he begins. He should look at students in turn as if talking to each personally, speaking slowly and clearly. To avoid a soporific monotone he must use effectively the 'Five Ps'. He must speak conversationally but vary Pitch (inflection), Power and Pace, while Phrasing logically and using the telling Pause to underline points and give his listeners time to assimilate his words. To avoid being a tailor's dummy he must use gesture and facial expression.

To claim attention he must have something to say, say it lucidly, and say it with confidence, fluency, enthusiasm, humour and attack; and, like that doyen of national coaches, Warwick Shute, he must be a bit of a showman, but never a long-winded bore. He should always prepare, practise and time all exposition. Preferably in the bath!

PERSONALITY

The rock foundation is, of course, an unquenchable, obvious, bubbling enthusiasm. To this he must add a ready approachability and sociability and a nearly limitless patience and encouragement for the duffer, the beginner and the unco-ordinated. With better players, he should know when and how to upbraid, be critical, drive, yet even in his student's defeat find something to praise. He must not suffer fools gladly; he must be prepared to put the awkward, the lazy and unreceptive, or the hair-splitter brusquely in his place. A touch of humour is an excellent spice (Plate 54).

He must be able to deal with emergencies such as failure of shuttles to arrive or the sudden loss of a court. He must not be too dogmatic or didactic, or too ready to crush all unorthodoxy. He must enjoy forever experimenting with new approaches to suit different students. He must be able to organize large groups quickly. He must be something of a perfectionist. But it is by his obvious love and enjoyment of the game that he will teach most.

KNOWLEDGE OF GAME

A coach should obviously have a wide knowledge of every aspect of the game and of its laws. Badminton is slowly but steadily building up its own literature, largely on tactics and techniques. He should make a point of reading the *Badminton Gazette* so that he is acquainted with the general badminton scene, latest coaching techniques, and new equipment. Much also can be learnt not only from fellow badminton coaches on refresher courses, but also from coaches in other sports. No opportunity should be lost of watching the leading modern players.

EXPOSITION

All this knowledge, no matter how persuasively put over, will be useless if it is not expounded clearly and logically. A coach should be able to break down strokes into their sequential parts. Tactics too must be developed slowly and logically. He should learn something of teaching methods, of learning, revision, retention, and mental processes. With exposition must go the ability to use carefully phrased questions (see p. 21).

PLAYING ABILITY

Ideally, a county or national coach has played first-class badminton. Then, he will carry more prestige in the eyes of his group. He will also be able to demonstrate practically that what he says theoretically is indeed true. He will be able to bring out latent weaknesses for strengthening and to give practice in any type of game his student is likely to meet.

In the ranks of club coaches, it is enough if he can demonstrate all shots well in cold blood, feed accurately, and play well enough to join in a game to create desired tactical situations and opportunities for stroke play.

OTHER QUALITIES

He must inculcate his own deep urge to win but show that quixotically generous line decisions are as out of place as unfair ones. Nevertheless, he must be able to accept defeat with a smile, and victory with an uncondescending sympathy for the loser.

Fitness and good health are also important. An erect, alert and fit coach is an inspiration; a limp, lethargic, winded one cuts little ice (Plate 59). Another valuable quality is shrewd judgement in play and character evaluation. Early assessment of potential can save much heartache on both sides.

Finally the coach must have a sound philosophy. He must believe that there is more than mere enjoyment and excitement in playing badminton; that physical fitness helps meet crises not only on court but also in daily life. Health, strength and endurance are not qualities lightly to be discounted; and reasonable control of joy or despair on court helps create a stable personality. Mental activity must go hand in hand with physical activity both on and off court. Badminton channels youthful restlessness and energy from destructive to creative action. It is a form of self-expression for many who might not otherwise achieve it.

13

2

COACHING COURSES

The Badminton Association of England has a well organized coaching scheme. It runs courses to train would-be coaches. These are held at various venues throughout the country in consecutive or proximate weekends. The student thus obtains some 20 hours of coaching and practice; during this time he is continually assessed by the coach-assessors running the course (1 to each 8 players). There is no formal examination; he is told at the end of the course whether or not he has been successful. If he has failed, he is told the faults he must correct before a next attempt. Official qualification gives both the coach and his students assurance that 'he knows his stuff'. Moreover, it is essential if he wishes to be paid as an evening institute instructor and retain his amateur status!

SYLLABUSES

There are four grades of coach: Club, Advanced Club, County and National. The basic syllabus includes:
Stroke production
Tactical and positional play
Knowledge of the laws
Knowledge of coaching set-up
Fitness training
Club Coaches will be asked:
1. to coach an individual, and a group, in stroke production.
2. to coach 4 players in tactics.
3. to answer oral questions on the laws and further tactical points.
Advanced Club Coaches will do the same but to a higher standard.
County Coaches will also work to a higher standard; in addition,

14

they will have to coach a group of would-be coaches in coaching fundamentals.

National Coaches are elected by the Coaching Committee from the ranks of very experienced County Coaches; they must be prepared to coach anywhere in the country.

COURSES

A list of courses is printed in the first issue each season of the *Badminton Gazette*. Full details may be obtained also from the BA of E Coaching Secretary, Flt Lt O. A. Cussen, DFC, RAF (Retd), 44/45 Palace Road, Bromley, Kent BR1 3JU. Centres such as Crystal Palace, Orion Hall (London), Harlow, Bracknell, Yeovil, Lea Green (Matlock), University of Lancaster, and others in the Midlands and North, are chosen so that all regions are covered and travelling is kept to a minimum. These are held throughout the season. (The *Badminton Gazette*, published six times during the season, is available from the Editor, 66 St. Martin's Hill, Canterbury, Kent CT1 1PS. £1·50 post free.)

Courses for teachers who wish to gain a knowledge of coaching are also run by the English Schools' Badminton Association (Hon. Sec. D. H. Milford, address p. 16). This is not quite so exacting as the BA of E award, but it is run on very much the same lines. The ESBA award their own smart badge.

HOW TO PASS

Frank Smith, a National Coach and examiner, made the following points in an article in the *Badminton Gazette*:

Group Coaching: Forget the examiner! Then by being relaxed and human, just coach the group and work with them so that they enjoy it.

Voice, Personality and Appearance: Speak slowly and clearly; be yourself; be clean and neat.

Group Coaching: First quickly assess the group's standard by short games. Give a good demonstration. See that all the group are working; change them round regularly and spend time with each one. Correct their actual faults – not imaginary ones for which you do remember a remedy!

Coaching Individuals: Spot the errors then correct the basic one, without overworking the student, to show a real improvement.

Above all, the coach should know he is well prepared and has had reasonable experience. Let him remember he is told the strokes he has to coach half an hour before going on court. Examiners such as Frank are badminton enthusiasts and human beings who want to see what he knows and can do rather than to catch him out and mark down errors. Everyone makes a mistake or two; that will not fail him if the rest of his work is efficient.

WHERE THE QUALIFIED COACH IS NEEDED

Badminton is growing so popular that more and more coaches are needed in schools, clubs and evening institutes.

School PE teachers cannot be expert in all the many games now played in schools; they are, therefore, often glad of expert help. The English Schools' Badminton Association (Hon. Secretary, D. H. Milford, 24 Abbotswood Road, Streatham, London SW16 1AP) is always pleased to hear from qualified teacher-coaches who wish to coach outside their own schools.

All too seldom is a newly qualified coach an accepted prophet in his own club. Other clubs' needs can best be discovered by writing to the County Coaching Secretary. If his name and address cannot be learnt locally, the Secretary, Badminton Association of England, 44–45 Palace Road, Bromley, Kent BRI 3JU, can help.

Application for work in youth clubs and evening institutes is best made through the local education committee. Such classes are almost invariably paid, at rates varying between £3·00 and £3·50 per hour. This payment may be kept provided the coach is qualified and subject to provisions laid down in the BA of E handbook.

As he climbs the coaching ladder and sports a county or national badge, the Sports Council (formerly the CCPR) and BA of E will be equally glad of his services for a wide variety of coaching: series of weekly evening classes, weekend or week-long courses for beginners on holiday, for the advanced player, or for the would-be coach.

There is much work to be done. It is demanding and exacting, but it is great fun and most rewarding for the coach as he teaches other people to get the same joy from badminton that he himself does.

16

3

PUTTING A LESSON ACROSS

Apart from the general qualities mentioned in Chapter 1, the coach must also have a basic knowledge of educational principles, of learning and teaching. No matter what his playing skill, he will get little across to a class unless his teaching is effective.

LESSON NOTES

Only an experienced coach can give a lesson off the cuff. Initially, it is essential to prepare lesson notes. If they are set out clearly and succinctly in tabular form they will help clarify thoughts, prevent dreaded tongue-tied silences, serve as a record of work done, and be a reminder of errors to be avoided. He should always include a 'reserve' exercise – just in case he 'dries-up'.

CLASS

12 boys and girls. Age 14-16. Venue: Longbridge YC. (One court with wide surrounds.) 6 p.m. to 7 p.m. Previous knowledge : court markings; grip; high serve.

AIM

To teach the overhead forehand defensive clear to novices.

MATERIALS

8 racquets; 12 practice shuttles; 2 nets; 6 air-flow balls.

BLACKBOARD SUMMARY

DEFENSIVE CLEAR
Swing racquet back early between shoulder-blades.
Snap arm up straight: use wrist: 'throw!'
Impact: high above head.
Follow-through: long; on target.

INTRODUCTION

LINK
Recapitulation of high serve – this is how it is
returned. (2)

USE OF STROKE
Limits opponent's attack – gains time – opens-up court –
mainly in singles. (1)

INTEREST AROUSAL
(i) Foundation overhead stroke; (ii) power stroke; (iii)
easiest of three. (2)
Throwing action: class throw balls in pairs. (2)

DEVELOPMENT

DEMONSTRATION
As in singles (John Reed to come with me as feeder)
(i) Separate shots (ii) Rally. (2)

EXPOSITION
(i) Grip (ii) backswing (iii) forward swing (iv) impact
(v) follow-through (vi) recovery. Questions. (3)

SHADOWING
As fluent whole. (2)

PRACTICE
Organization: (i) positioning: 4 groups of 3, staggered
(ii) instructions to feeders and fags (iii) safety: 'Do' – not
'Don't'. (2)
Stroke Production: single strokes. Fag calls out target
score – last 10 to count. Change round every 5 minutes.
Summarize general errors. Questions. (15)

Diversion and Warmer: Agility practice in pairs, with balls, for footwork. (5)

Routine: 2 groups of 6. Coach and J. Reed feed players alternately for consecutive rally. Pass on racquets. Square running. Fig. 34 Point for each rally of 5 shots. Questions. (7)

Conditioned Game: Three 4's (each for 5 minutes). High serve and clear only. Non-players do fitness exercise or practise high serve to targets as team game. Questions. (15)

CONCLUSION

DEMONSTRATION AND RECAPITULATION
Singles serves and clears. (2)

HOMEWORK
Think, read, and shadow stroke. What other shots from the back line can be tried next week?

Coach talking and demonstrating, 13 minutes; students active, 47 minutes.

SELF-CRITICISM

The coach should honestly assess his successes and failures. If he writes them down on a page opposite the appropriate notes, they will stand him in good stead in subsequent lessons: e.g. 'Talked too fast', 'Cleared short in demonstration', 'Forgot use of wrist', 'Spent too long with some students', 'No time for recap'.

TAKING THE LESSON

CONDITIONS

Few halls are ideal for badminton. Heating, lighting, seating, changing accommodation, floor surface, and tea-break facilities must all be checked and, where necessary, improved, before a course starts. The best learning is done early under the best conditions.

EQUIPMENT

Having bought the best possible, the coach should ensure that a few minutes before the class is due to begin he has ready not only racquets and shuttles but also perhaps tennis balls, targets, chalk, air-flow balls, books, and visual aids as well as the vital tea, milk and sugar!

CLASS GROUPING

Well prepared, the coach can now start his lesson. He should place his students in a line or semicircle facing him so that all can see and hear him clearly. They should be with their backs to such possible distractions as another game, curvaceous blondes or burly he-men. During demonstration, all students should be able to see the striking arm and the point of impact and be allowed to move about for this purpose. In exposition and practices, he should spread and keep students well apart for safety; place left-handers on the left for forehand shots, on right for backhands. Students are spread in exposition so that they can make tentative attempts to translate the coach's words into physical actions (Plates 52 and 53).

VERBAL EXPLANATION

This, contrary to all too many coaches' ideas, is only a secondary method of learning. It is all important, however, to use both facets: pure exposition and questioning.

EXPOSITION

Tactics must be developed logically, stroke by stroke. Strokes, so long played automatically by the coach, must be mentally and verbally rehearsed sequentially so that both correct phrasing and detail are achieved, and, after an arresting introduction, put across freshly and interestingly.

That live-wire tennis coach, John Crook (from whom I have learnt so much, not merely of badminton but of music), used to tell youngsters to boo him if he talked longer than sixty seconds. I have a slightly higher opinion of their word-resistance: three to five minutes. But as in everything else it depends on the age and ability of the group, and each group varies. With youngsters, simplicity, absence of jargon, and lack of any possible ambiguity are essentials.

Adults will listen rather longer but often five minutes' talk is twice, not half, as effective as ten; for a spate of detail leaves

20

the group floundering, and few people efficiently assimilate more than two or three new ideas at a time. Words are best used to explain when a stroke is used or to correct errors. Explanation of principles does not immediately help technique but may aid in its retention.

With both child and adult, exposition should decrease after the initial explanation. Self-instruction and discovery of error, fostered by a willingness to experiment, slowly become more important. The learner learns more by doing than by listening.

Though the voice should be used sparingly it should be 'played' as effectively as a musical instrument, with every possible variation of pitch, power, pace, pause – and a certain amount of gesture.

QUESTIONING

It is to be hoped that this heading does not smack too much of the secret police! Nevertheless, it is the essential complement of exposition. By it, the coach finds out his students' previous knowledge and so knows where to start his exposition. He can also use it to find out how successful his exposition has been: how much has been grasped and how well. It is a means of holding the group's attention (for even adults do not like to be caught napping), and of giving them a feeling of participation. Above all, it makes a student think for himself.

Such questions must be skilfully phrased to elicit only the required information. So too they must be tactfully posed for few adults wish to do a 'Vice Versa' and revert to their school days! The question should always be asked of the group so that all are forced to think. After a brief pause, a specific student should be indicated; in this way even the shyest are brought into the discussion. The 'thruster' must not hog all the answers!

'Student participation' is a *cri de coeur* of modern educationalists. It will be appreciated by younger students but older ones often feel they are not getting their money's worth if they do not get a certain amount of solid exposition from the maestro himself. If badly done, such questioning can be confusing and time-wasting; if well done, it keeps a group on its mental toes and gives essential variety.

DEMONSTRATION

Many students learn better through the eye than the ear. For the coach, playing a stroke automatically in the heat of a game is

21

very different from playing it in cold blood before students. He will do well to practise his demonstrations, for a fluent one creates a lasting impression.

He must demonstrate according to the book even if he himself does not always play to it. Each stroke should be played from the correct part of the court, not in limbo, but in the tactical context of a rally. Drops must not be played from midcourt to a lone feeder but from the base line with a 'partner' at the net and two 'opponent-feeders' on mid-court bases, making or simulating lob returns. First, individual shots are played and allowed to drop to the ground. Then a rally of consecutive shots is played. Finally, the object of the exercise is shown: in this case to elicit a short lob which is 'killed'. However, tactical considerations must not obscure stroke technique; the former should be the backcloth against which the latter is better displayed.

Such a demonstration may be given silently or with commentary. Alternatively, the students' attention can be drawn (by questions) to the vital points of the stroke as it is played : 'Where is the point of impact?' or 'How are the feet positioned?' They should also be encouraged to watch follow-through and recovery rather than the shuttle's flight. To ensure success, the student-feeder should be carefully briefed. If the students are absolute beginners, hand-feeding will have to be resorted to or a friend brought along.

It is always wise to have an unashamed knock before the demonstration. Should the latter go wrong even then, perhaps through nervousness, the coach must not be panicked into abandoning it. He must admit his failure and by greater concentration succeed; in so doing he underlines a secret of success. When all goes well, he must avoid the temptation of enjoying himself but boring his students by a lengthy 'single'.

Should the coach be a poor demonstrator, he must bring a friend to demonstrate or use good loop films. Occasional use of a skilled pupil as demonstrator arouses interest and boosts motivation. While students' good and bad points may be analysed by the group, a student should never be asked to demonstrate faults (Plate 54).

SHADOWING

After the demonstration, if there has been no commentary, the coach may wish to shadow the stroke; that is to break it into its parts (backswing, forward swing and impact, follow-through and recovery) one by one, as he details the technique. He will then get his students to imitate him, either in one fluent action, or in parts before weaving them into a whole. This allows full concentration on a difficult technique without overloading the student still further with the added terrors (I use the word advisedly in relation to beginners) of movement and timing (Plate 52).

PRACTICE

So important and detailed is this aspect of coaching that it has been dealt with at length in Chapter 10.

ANALYSIS AND CORRECTION

This is dealt with in detail in Chapter 9, but it will not be out of place to deal with fundamentals here.

ANALYSIS

The coach should position himself unobtrusively where he can best see action and impact. A beginner aware of scrutiny by the Omnipotent becomes as relaxed as a steel bar. If a fault is not obvious, a coach should systematically (but with delicacy!) run his eye over the student. In turn, he should check each part of the body : feet, trunk, hand, arm, wrist and eye; or each part of the stroke : backswing, forward swing, impact, follow-through and recovery. He should learn to watch the action rather than the shuttle's flight, save in so far as it reveals poor length or trajectory. He should quietly wait to see which errors recur, then pick out the one which may well be the root cause of the others. A late backswing will cause short backswing, bent arm and lack of power at one fell swoop.

CORRECTION

The coach should quietly and quickly correct the error before feeder and fags as well as striker. Thus they too will learn and not be bored by an apparently intimate *tête à tête*. The error may be explained verbally, by question or exposition, or by shadowing and demonstration. It may assist the striker if he shadows the stroke before again hitting the shuttle. Manual guidance also helps : this is the coach actually moving the student's arm through the correct action, either in shadowing or in an actual shot. (The latter is not as difficult as it sounds!) Fig. 56.

Occasionally an error is largely or partly due to bad feeding; this too must be remedied. Sometimes the coach can help timing by calling 'Back', 'Reach UP', 'Right foot across', and so on at the crucial moment. The coach should watch a few more shots before leaving with a last succinct repetition of the correction – and an encouraging word.

RETENTION

Neither techniques nor tactics will be remembered *in toto* after a single lesson. Indeed, in my early days of teaching, my youthful ideals were sadly jarred when an elderly, and by now thoroughly misanthropic, colleague used to inform his class quite frankly: 'Teaching you is like throwing muck against the stable wall; 99% drops to the ground.' (And that despite the fact that he wielded a very pretty chair leg!) Recapitulation and revision must therefore be frequent.

During a lesson, the same idea will have to be repeated several times. Since this is for the benefit of those students upon whom the previous explanations made no impact it is essential to approach it from a different angle and in different words. If, 'the right arm should be straight at impact in the overhead clear' does not ring a bell, try 'throw the racquet up hard so that it hurts a bit in the elbow joint' or 'try and touch the girders with your racquet' or 'you want to hammer in that almost out-of-reach nail'. Homely analogies and allusions often do the trick.

Time must always be left at the end of a lesson for a final recapitulation. Only then, with a correct picture in his mind, can the student do his homework of mental learning correctly. This recapping can be done by (a) summing up (b) eliciting main points or (c) a final demonstration; and in the following weeks quick recaps will act both as links and as aids to revision.

VISUAL AIDS

Realizing how important a part the eye plays in learning, the modern coach makes all possible use of visual aids. Badminton unfortunately is not blessed with many good films. RSL loan rather old ones of Thomas Cup matches, and of the great Ken Davidson and Wong Peng Soon playing and coaching. The only good modern film available is that of Judy Hashman's thrilling and remarkable tenth victory in the All-England Singles in 1967. It can be hired from the BA of E Coaching Secretary as can loops on stroke production by that very great player Tony Jordan.

Loops are best appreciated on a spectro-analyser, which can project the film slowly frame by frame or stop on one frame for pinpoint analysis. Equally invaluable (and even more expensive) is the video-tape which enables a player to be filmed and within seconds to see the film played back. Photographs from the *Badminton Gazette* can be projected by an epidiascope.

The photographically minded coach can find pleasure and profit in making his own films and transparencies. They are excellent stimulants: players love to see themselves in action – and the camera will be believed!

4

COACHING IN SCHOOLS AND EVENING INSTITUTES

All that has been written in previous chapters still applies, but this type of coaching does pose the additional problems of large numbers of students and their relative lack of ability or fitness. For a single court, numbers should be restricted to a maximum of twenty if real progress and enjoyment are to be achieved. For purely stroke practice sessions it is possible to squeeze in as many as twenty-four to thirty students. In both cases, mass coaching is the only answer, far from ideal but much better than nothing.

COACHING IN SCHOOLS

In a school it is often impossible to accept all pupils wishing to play because of other demands on the gym. All too frequently, play is restricted to sixth-formers to give them at least a taste of the game before they leave. This, however, can often be done on the various school leavers' courses organized by the LEA.

It is much more vital that the coach runs a junior section. Then the 11-plus children have time to develop into able players and the really talented ones to reach the top of the junior ladder. As they mature, they should be encouraged to join adult clubs (though not to the detriment of their examinations). Most one-court clubs are only too glad to find a source of ready trained youngsters. In return, they may be able to help with provision of old shuttles and racquets as well as giving a little coaching advice if needed. This extra play with adults is essential for most youngsters if they are to mature rapidly. Gillian Gilks, then a member of Wimbledon BC, played for England while still at school!

They should be given every chance to reach the top in competitive junior badminton. Many counties have a schools' association run solely by teachers. The first Hon. Secretary of the English Schools' Association was Len Wright, who did a tremendous job in organizing an inter-county tournament and even full international matches. Margaret Beck, who toured South Africa when still only seventeen, would be the first to admit that she owes much to him, as she does to that great enthusiast and national coach, Charles Cumpstey. David Milford now carries on the good work (p. 16).

In addition, nearly every senior county association organizes its own junior section. League and county matches are played; coaching is organized; and county junior championships lead to the great event of the season, held early in January at Wimbledon BC, the All-England Junior Championships. This is often the stepping stone to the top senior honours. And 1969 saw, for the first time, a highly successful European Junior Championship.

In addition, the Sports Council (70 Brompton Rd, London SW3) runs holiday courses for under-eighteens. The BA of E offers an annual award of a place on such a course to a very promising youngster; this was made possible by the will of that great-hearted Surrey player and administrator, Bill Wiltshire.

As to the running of such a school club, teachers will need little guidance from me. I would, however, like to make one or two suggestions. The formal 'teacher aspect' should be left in the classroom so far as is consistent with the maintenance of the unobtrusive discipline essential for safety and organization. Steam can be let off quickly with a fitness, running, or ball co-ordination exercise. Activity, enjoyment and competition must be the key words.

Methods of coaching will vary according to the numbers, type of child, and the coach's inclination. It may be done:

1. Largely by the coach's demonstration and the briefest of exposition, followed by shadowing and practice.

2. Setting the children a task (e.g. hitting the shuttle from end to end of the court), and allowing them to experiment for themselves, to observe and discuss the efforts of others, and then to select the best technique.

3. By more formal exposition.

In each case, use can be made of children's eagerness to help one another, i.e. a miniature monitorial system. Practices should be interspersed with competitive team games. Care of equipment, sportsmanship, and court courtesies should be inculcated from the start.

COACHING IN EVENING INSTITUTES

Adults in evening classes are a rather different proposition. If the neatly marked register is not to show an ever-growing toll of absences and finally of resignations, many points must be borne in mind or the class may well be cancelled. Remember, other classes call them; turning out on a winter's night can be irksome; and they are not naturals, for them it is hard work. Success must be achieved early and progressively. Be sociable, not Olympian, and chat with your group in the changing room and at tea break; create the best hall conditions; play in whites and encourage others to do the same; use 'pop' music with a strong beat in footwork exercises; have plenty of round games; encourage competition; set up a simple keep-fit circuit; see that your students have the fun of games or conditioned games as soon as possible; give praise unstintingly; without clowning, use humour; find out why your students have enrolled, and use this motivation to the full. Regard regular absentees as your failure, not theirs. Never succumb to the temptation of jettisoning coaching and allowing your class to become a club under your administration. Remember you are paid to coach, with all that that implies.

A further problem arises with evening institute classes. What happens to the player you have made? Too often the cry is, 'I can't find a club that will take me.' If that player gives up badminton, your time and public money have both been grossly wasted. Do not forget your students after the last session; they are still your responsibility until they are happily settled in a club.

You have three alternatives:

1. Start intermediate or advanced classes.
2. Through your county coaching secretary, make contact with local clubs.
3. With the backing of your students, found a new club.

HOW TO START WITH BEGINNERS

The coach should first show the student how to hold the racquet (Plate 2a). Confidence in being able to hit the shuttle at all is next established by each player having a shuttle and hitting a rally of successive shots upwards off his own racquet. After this they can hit underhand one to another. They should now be able to attempt the high serve.

Next follows throwing practice. Then comes the clear with the racquet (for some at least) started from between the shoulderblades, i.e. no preliminary backswing. This is gradually lengthened so that when the full stroke can be played confidently, the student can strive for greater length (Plates 57 and 58).

These practices are interspersed with co-ordination ball games and agility exercises. Easy arm- and wrist-strengthening exercises should also be introduced. Within a couple of weeks, the first simple conditioned game (high serves and clears only) can be played.

In the next seven or eight weeks the other strokes should be introduced, one leading to another in technique, and tactically fitting into the badminton jigsaw. As a rough idea of most of the strokes is acquired, ordinary games as well as conditioned ones can be played, but with little additional tactical detail added.

Explanation of court-markings, scoring, and rules, as well as chats on equipment and the wider field of badminton, should be brought in gradually as relevant. Each week there should be constant quick recaps and practising of strokes already taught.

SPECIMEN SYLLABUS

FIRST TERM (13 weeks)

1. Forehand grip. Hitting up. Hitting up in pairs. High serve. Overhead clear.
2. High serve and clear. Slow drops. Forehand lobs (or under-arm clears).
3. High serve and clear. Slow drops and lobs.
4. Fast drops and backhand lobs. Backhand grip.
5. Smash. Lob and push returns.
6. Smash. Lob and push returns. Dab net shots.
7. General revision and testing.
8. Overhead shots. Low serve and upward net shot return.
9. Overhead shots. Low serve and downward push return.
10. Forehand and backhand drives.
11. Low serve. Drives and pushes. Net interceptions.
12. General revision and testing.
13. General revision. American tournament.

SECOND TERM (13 weeks)

Basic strokes are revised and practised again to higher standards of length and consistency. As these improve the simple basic tactics already touched on are expanded. Additional strokes such as flick and drive serves and overhead backhand clears and drops can be brought in if warranted.

1. High serve and clear. Singles tactics.
2. High serve. Drop shot and lob. Singles tactics.
3. High serve. Smash and returns. Singles tactics.
4. Low serve and returns. Flick serve. Mixed tactics.
5. Low serve and returns. Drive serve and round-the-head smash. Mixed tactics.
6. Drives. 'Danish Wipe'. Men's and ladies' doubles tactics.
7. General revision and testing.
8. Net shots. Overhead backhand clear. Doubles tactics.
9. Net shots. Overhead backhand clear and drop shot. Doubles tactics.
10. Overhead and complementary strokes.
11. Underarm and side-arm strokes.
12. General revision and testing.
13. General revision. American tournament.

SPECIMEN LESSON

7.00 p.m. Ball bouncing in pairs for agility and co-ordination.
7.05 p.m. Clears: (a) practice for style and length; (b) rallying in pairs.
7.15 p.m. Drops and lobs. Rallying in teams or against coach.
7.25 p.m. Low serve.
7.40 p.m. Upward net return of low serve.
7.50 p.m. Shuttle runs.
7.55 p.m. Break.
8.00 p.m. Conditioned games (only drops, clears and lobs allowed). Others practise low serve and return round court in vacant spaces.
8.20 p.m. Maze runs.
8.25 p.m. Games (eleven up). Coach talks to others on rules and badminton news. Low serve and return or other strokes practised round court.
8.55 p.m. Recap and demonstration of low serve and return.
Homework: 'Thinking' shot. Reading in book. Practice indoors or in garden. (Low serve.)

TESTS

Some exercises should be purely for experiment and practice;

others, right from the outset, should be motivated by test-scoring. For example, the last five shots of a practice should be at target lengths and areas. (Shuttles must be of standard speed.) Scores should be recorded on a large sheet of drawing paper (Fig. 1).

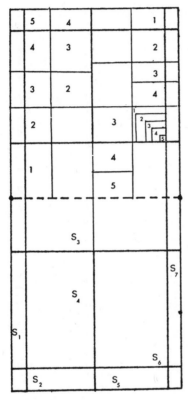

Fig. 1. Court test markings: S_1 plays drives or Danish 'Wipes' and S_2 clears; S_3 lobs and S_4 high serves; S_5 plays slow drops; S_6 smashes; S_7 serves low.

Similarly, every six weeks, a cumulative test may be given. Success takes a player from Ungraded to Grade 1. Target areas for each stroke are marked out on the court in chalk. Strikers stand on correct bases for different strokes and play each stroke five times. Shots missed, hit into net, or out of court count as a stroke but obviously gain no points. Feeding is done by the students by hand or racquet; strikers can refuse poorly fed shots.

31

The figures given below for Grades 5 to 2 show the pass mark for each activity. In each grade, players should pass in at least five or six of these, according to class standard.

Points are scored for each shot as shown on the marked court in Fig. 1. Each shuttle run scores a point (see page 136).

	1st Term			
	Grade 5		Grade 4	
	After 6 weeks		After 12 weeks	
	Men	Ladies	Men	Ladies
Shuttle run (cross-court)	12	8	14	10
Shuttle run (up and down)	9	6	11	8
High serve	10	10	14	14
Low serve	—	—	10	10
Clear	12	8	15	10
Drops	10	9	14	12
Smash	8	6	10	8
Backhand drive	—	—	12	7

	2nd Term			
	Grade 3		Grade 2	
	After 18 weeks		After 24 weeks	
	Men	Ladies	Men	Ladies
High serve	16	16	18	18
Low serve	12	12	14	14
Clear	8(3)	8(2)	12(3)	12(2)
Drop	4(3)	4(3)	7(4)	7(4)
Lob	4(2)	4(2)	7(2)	7(2)
Smash	10	8	12	10
Danish wipe	12	9	14	11

In 2nd term tests, low serve must pass below a cord stretched 12-15 inches above tape (Grade 3), and 9-12 inches above tape (Grade 2). Figures for clears, drops and lobs are number of strokes played consecutively and (in brackets) the minimum length to which they must be played, i.e. Clear 8(3) = 8 con-

1

1 The Author with four of England's leading internationals, Ray Sharp, Margaret Allen, Sue Whetnall and Paul Whetnall, all from his own county, Kent. At his request, they are sporting their well earned England blazers

3

GRIPS

2a Forehand: Sue Whetnall's fingers are spread out; V between thumb and forefinger pointing down shaft; butt end of racquet on heel of hand

2b Backhand: thumb now flat and almost straight down broad bevel

3 Frying-pan: racquet face square to net – for use at net only

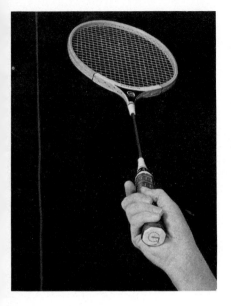

4a

4b

5

USE OF WRIST
4a Wrist cocked back

4b Wrist and arm in straight line

5 Wrist fully uncocked and brought over

6

7

SMASH
6 Paul Whetnall, body bending back, left arm upraised as counterbalance, steps back to position himself perfectly

7 As he steps back he swings his racquet up over his shoulder and then down between shoulder-blades

8   9

8 Racquet now being strongly snapped up again; body turning square to net as Paul seeks for height

9 Impact: arm straight, wrist uncocking, impact in front of head, right foot swinging through, eyes on shuttle

10

11

JUMPING SMASH
10 Ray launches himself vertically upwards like a miniature Apollo rocket to achieve quick return and steep angle; racquet head is down between shoulderblades

11 One point landing: wrist well over; weight swinging forward on to right foot for instant recovery

12 Girls can do it too! Tyna Barinaga, US Singles Champion, just going airborne

13   14

ROUND-THE-HEAD SMASHES

13 Here Paul Whetnall intercepts the shuttle higher than in 14 but still wide of the head; body beautifully arched

14 Weight coming down on outstretched, braced left leg, he leans right over, with wrist cocked and bent arm, to sweep racquet just above head for impact to left of it

secutive clears, none falling short of Square 3. Drop 4(3) = 4 consecutive drops, none falling deeper than square 3. (3 tries allowed.) Coach acts as feeder.

FINAL TEST (Grade 1)
Three minute single with coach who assesses strokes, tactics, movement, accuracy and consistency, each out of a possible 10 marks, making 50 in all; 30 is a pass.

UTILIZATION OF FLOOR SPACE
One of the main criticisms of badminton by school and Further Education PE Organizers is that too much space is occupied by too few active performers. They point out that one gym can be properly used by a dozen basketball or volleyball players, trampolinists, gymnasts, or fencers, but by only four badminton players. This idea is completely erroneous. Up to thirty players can be usefully and actively engaged in worthwhile badminton practices in the average one-court hall or even the smallest school gym (60ft by 30ft). This can be done in any one of a number of ways or by a combination of them.

HITTING AGAINST WALLS
Here, there are two possible methods. In one, well spaced hand-feeders and fags keep up a steady supply of shuttles to the striker, who hits them at the wall. Net-lines and targets on the walls make for realism and competition.

In the other, the player feeds himself by rallying against the wall (lobs, clears, drives, and even smashes and returns). He counts his longest consecutive rally (Fig. 2). Plastic shuttles stand this form of punishment best. If hit with plenty of wrist, they rebound far enough from the wall to allow a reasonably full backswing. (The walls of the Drill Hall in Nottingham probably still bear traces of the author's indefatigable juvenile prowess in this direction!)

USE OF SHUTTLE FAGS
To occupy large numbers and to speed up production, two or three shuttle fags can be added to the feeder and striker already on court. No. 1 stands behind the striker; No. 2, at the net; No. 3, behind or near the feeder. They carefully retrieve shuttles

and throw them back with the appropriate action. They also learn by watching the striker and by being brought in to hear

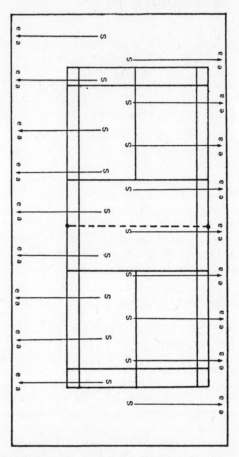

Fig. 2. Class hitting against walls: Class is divided into threes: S = striker; e = feeder; a = fag.

the coach's comments to him. When the strikers' turns finish, all students should face one way before moving round, one place, anti-clockwise (Fig. 3).

PRACTICE ROUTINES

As students improve, the fags may be turned into players. In groups of four, each one then plays a different shot as it might

34

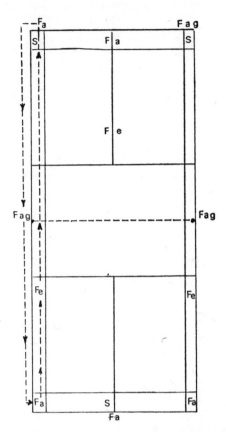

Fig. 3. Clearing or dropping or smashing practice; 14 players occupied. As each player has his turn as striker, he moves anti-clockwise to another position.

occur in a real rally. Thus, three or even four groups of four may simultaneously practise any of the following routines, not necessarily the same routine each (Fig. 4 and Plate 55).

1. A serves high to C; C smashes at B; B plays push return; D attempts to intercept.

2. E serves low to F; F plays push return to G, E's partner; G plays another push return which H, F's partner, intercepts.

3. J and K drive and push flat at each other; L and M at net, attempt interceptions.

4. N serves high to P; P plays a drop shot; Q plays a net shot; R lobs to N, who starts the sequence again in reverse by playing a drop shot.

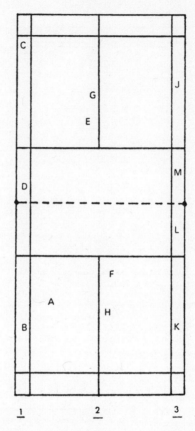

Fig. 4. Practice routines: twelve players on one court learning different skills.

RUNNING-ROUND EXERCISES

A large number of these can be devised in which teams of players take it in turn to hit the shuttle. To make the practice less static, each player, after his shot, runs on a predetermined 'course' before rejoining the end of his team. Large numbers can be kept occupied actively and competitively. Feeding can be done in a variety of ways. See page 116.

PLAYING ACROSS THE WIDTH OF THE HALL

In this way, if three nets are strung down the length of the hall, a court 60ft wide is made. Allowing 6 feet between

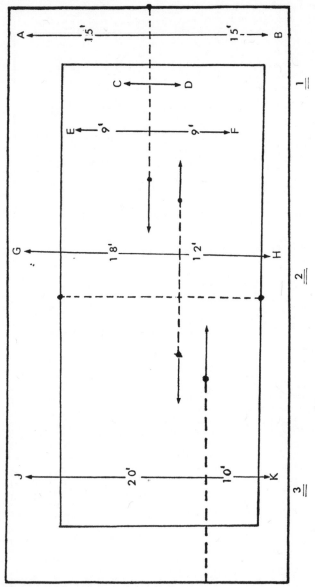

Fig. 5. Playing across width of hall: (1) With net 15 ft from walls: A and B drive; C and D play net shots; E and F practise serve and return. (2) With net 18 ft from back wall: G and H practise smash and return respectively. (3) With net 20 ft from back wall: J and K practise drop and lob respectively. Nets will be strung down whole length of hall with net positioned as in 1 or 2 or 3.

37

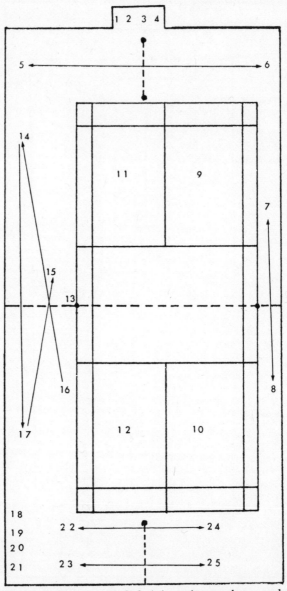

Fig. 6. Utilizing all floor space: 1, 2, 3, 4, in equipment alcove, read *Badminton Complete* or discuss tactics on pegboard; 5 and 6 drive; 7 and 8 low serve; 9, 10, 11 and 12 play game; 13 scores, 14 smashes, 15 net interception, 16 high serves, 17 push return; 18, 19, 20, 21 do fitness exercises (wall-bars, Sargent jump etc); 22, 23, 24, 25 play flat pushes, net-shots, services etc.

players, this means ten pairs can practise. Admittedly the court is now only 30ft long but except in clearing rallies, pair practices do not use the full length of the court. Thus, complementary strokes can be played if the position of the nets is slightly adjusted. In a gym 60ft by 40ft, still more room may be allotted (Fig. 5).

1. Drops fly 20-22ft to the net and are lob-returned from 2-6ft beyond it. (28ft used; net 20ft from the wall.)

2. Smashes fly 18ft to the net and are returned from 12ft beyond it. (30ft used; net 18ft from the wall.)

3. Net shots can be played with 6ft on either side of the net. (12ft used; net 15ft from wall.)

4. Service flies 9ft to net and is returned by player 9ft beyond it whose shot in turn may be returned by server's partner. (24ft used; net 15ft from wall.)

5. Drives and pushes may be played from and to 15ft beyond the net. (30ft used; net 15ft from wall.)

UTILIZING SPACE ROUND THE COURT

This can be done when you wish to keep the whole group busy, though four of them are using the court itself for a game. Practices can be devised so that all the court surrounds are usefully employed. Up to twenty-four players can work at one time, depending on the layout of the hall (Fig. 6).

MAINTAINING INTEREST

While play on court is always the prime interest, any of the following can be used as additional stimuli:

1. A visit to a local tournament, league or county match, or to the All-England Championships at Wembley Pool in March.

2. Tactical games played on a miniature court made of pegboard.

3. Design of posters to illustrate stroke production or tactics.

4. An evening of films, loops or ciné-film.

5. Making a scrapbook from results and photographs in the local and national press and the *Badminton Gazette*.

6. American tournaments, preferably one in which each player plays with a different partner against different opponents.

7. Sealed handicap tournaments, i.e. each pair are given a number of points to be added to the total number they actually score. This number is not revealed until the end of the tourna-

ment: consequently every pair has to play all out to gain every possible point.

8. A Novelty tournament. In this, handicaps which create a lot of fun are of this type:
(a) Partners tied together by a 15ft cord.
(b) Tennis or squash racquets replace badminton racquets.
(c) Each player has a black patch over one eye.
(d) Each player wears crash helmet and goggles or holds umbrella.

9. General badminton quiz.

10. Watching a badminton match on television.

11. Ladder contest: players' names are listed one below the other. Any player (or pair) may challenge one not more than three places above. If successful, the former moves above the latter; if unsuccessful, the player (or pair) may not challenge the winners again for a fortnight.

12. 'Tactical Talks' or 'Any Questions'. Bring in four local experts as panel.

13. Keeping of badminton diaries: the player's own results; his opponents' strengths and weaknesses.

14. Formation of a badminton library: Players give or lend badminton books to form a club library.

15. Establishment of camera club to take ciné and still films for coaching purposes.

5

EQUIPMENT

Choice of equipment both for a group and an individual student is very important; the best that can be afforded should be bought.

RACQUETS

Metal-framed Racquets. These, ranging in weight from 3.4 ozs to 5 ozs, are very tightly strung with nylon; they are, therefore, highly manoeuvrable and can be swung very fast, but their lack of weight somewhat nullifies the increased speed of swing in producing greater power. It also necessitates adjustment in playing touch shots such as low serves and net shots.

Conventional Racquets. The best ones, made by Dunlop and other famous firms, have ash frames, steel or fibre-glass shafts, and are strung with gut. Look for a non-slip grip of the right size, a shaft with a slight whip, and a racquet that is well balanced, not handle-heavy (Plate 2a).

Always keep racquets in a press in a cool, dry atmosphere. Protect them against rain. Never throw them about or scoop up shuttles with them.

SHUTTLES

Plastic. These cost about 11p.–20p. each and last for many hours before the nylon 'skirt' cracks or the rubber base becomes detached. They are a real economy for practices involving hard hitting by large numbers. Despite research and improvement, however, they still do not fly or 'feel' quite like a feathered shuttle and so are used comparatively little in better competitive play.

Feathered. Prices range from 25p. to 45p. They are easily damaged: a feather broken, the weight lost, or the kid base

41

cut. Few will last longer than an hour.

Their speeds are in grains weight: the lightest 77/78 are suitable for small one-court halls; 82/83 may be necessary in larger, cold halls where air resistance is greater.

Keep them in a cool, slightly damp room; dryness makes the feathers brittle by evaporating the natural oils. Frequently smooth ruffled feather-barbs between forefinger and thumb. NEVER allow students to scoop or to hit them on the half-volley along the floor.

CLOTHES

These should be made of a white absorbent material, loose enough and brief enough not to hamper breathing, body or racquet movement. Having sufficient sets permits a refreshing change after a hard game. Track suits give warmth, so reducing the possibility of muscle injury while helping to ensure early ease of movement.

Footwear is vitally important. Woollen, well talced socks help to prevent blisters. Shoes, fitting well and lacing up the instep, should be as light as possible commensurate with having a sorbo inner sole, a strong toe-cap, and a rough outer sole.

The well prepared player will carry with him to the courtside a light bag containing such small but important adjuncts as shoelaces, safety-pins, glucose, spectacle demisting agent, talc, salt tablets, etc. 'Sticky' customers will find a small hand towel in the pocket and a wrist-pad helpful. A bandeau or handkerchief enables the long-haired or bespectacled to have clear vision.

POSTS AND NETS

The most effective posts screw into the floor (doing away with decapitating guy lines) and have a pawl and ratchet attachment for height adjustment (5ft at centre; 5ft 1in. at side line).

Nets should be $\frac{3}{4}$in. mesh bound at the top with a doubled 3in. white band through which runs a suitable draw-cord. (A 24ft net allows another pair on court for group practices.)

COURTS AND MARKING

Slippery floors are the bane of good badminton. Wealthy clubs have an easily portable PVC felt-backed court surface on which white lines are marked on a green ground. Poorer ones (the majority) finely spray the floor with light paraffin oil (cost: about 20p.). Where permanent lines are not allowed, plastic adhesive tape can be used, taken up and relaid; obtainable in a variety of colours in 25yd rolls and five are needed (Fig. 7).

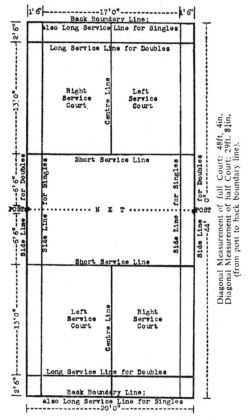

Fig. 7. Court dimensions and nomenclature (*reproduced by courtesy of BA of E.*)

LIGHTING

The most effective lighting consists of six 150 watt pearl lamps in a white non-reflecting back-board (8ft by 2ft), 13ft above each post and 2ft outside it. If necessary, butter muslin will obscure glare. Shining or light-coloured end walls can be cheaply covered by dark hessian curtains on draw pulleys.

6

BASIC TECHNIQUES

These are the very rock foundations of success. Their constant study and practice will pay handsome dividends, for only the synchronized use of feet, legs, body, fingers, wrist, arm and eye will give fluent stroke production. (In this, and following chapters, it is assumed that the reader is right-handed – and male!)

THE GRIP

The way a racquet is held is as important as the way it is swung to play a stroke. A faulty grip leads to faulty stroke production, and should, therefore, never be regarded as only a minor matter; it is fundamental.

All strokes can be played with the one basic grip. There are, however, special grips that may be used (a) for backhand shots; (b) for pushing and dabbing strokes at the net.

BASIC GRIP

This may be attained in different ways :

1. Player holds his racquet by its throat in his left hand, at right-angles to the floor. He places his right hand, with fingers outspread, on the strings. He draws this hand down the shaft to the handle. When the 'heel' of his hand reaches the butt-end of his racquet, he curls his fingers round the grip.

2. Player places his racquet on the floor. He picks it up as though he were going to 'chop wood' with the edge of the frame.

3. One player, holding another's racquet by the head, parallel and at right angles to the floor, proffers its handle to the owner. The latter 'shakes hands' with it.

Whichever way this basic grip is arrived at, check that:

44

(a) V between thumb and forefinger runs down centre (approximately) of side bevel of handle: this allows full use of of wrist.

(b) No length of handle protrudes beyond the hand: if it does (i) a couple of vital inches of reach are lost (ii) with a shortened 'lever', power is lost and (iii) use of wrist is inhibited.

(c) See that fingers are slightly spread, not bunched; and that the handle lies along the base of the fingers, not fully in the palm. This ensures that the racquet is gripped in the fingers rather the palm: delicacy of touch and 'feel' are thereby achieved.

(d) The racquet is now a direct continuation of the arm (Plate 2a).

BACKHAND GRIP

The player holds the racquet in his basic grip. By relaxing this, he can roll it in his fingers some 30° to his right. He can now place his thumb flat on and most straight down the back bevel. This gives him extra power and control, if he turns his wrist slightly to the left to 'open' the racquet face again (Plate 2b.)

FRYING-PAN GRIP

This too can be taken from the basic grip. This time the racquet is rolled a full 90° to the right. The racquet face is now square to the net with the V roughly down the back level (Plate 3).

This grip must not be used except to hit down at the net as it inhibits full use of the wrist. It is, however, useful at the net as it (a) helps player avoid hitting net; (b) enables shots to be played on both sides of him without change of grip or face of racquet; (c) enables shots to be angled rather more easily to the right.

Whichever grip is used, the racquet should be held firmly at impact but in a slightly relaxed grip between shots. This enables a quick change to be made from one grip to another. In power shots, the controlled tightening of the grip late in the forward swing adds speed to the head of the racquet in addition to that generated by arm and wrist.

Do not teach all these grips in one session or confusion will result. Teach the last two only when dealing with backhand shots and net shots respectively.

BASIC FAULTS

1. Racquet gripped too tightly: tension and jerkiness result.
2. Basic grip changes to frying pan because player turns

racquet in hand instead of turning his wrist to bring racquet head square to shuttle.

3. Fingers not spread out: clumsy, palm grip results.

In each case there will also be a loss of vital wrist flexibility.

PRACTICES

1. Let players rally gently, concentrating on grip.
(a) Get them to check grip regularly:
(b) Call 'Stop' in middle of rallying—then check grips.
2. When backhand is learnt:
(a) Off court, practise rolling racquet from forehand to backhand grip and back;
(b) Make students slowly hit shuttle underhand to partners' forehand and backhand; partners change grip appropriately.
3. When net shots are learnt:
(a) as in 2(a) but add frying-pan grip to sequence;
(b) still off court, coach calls out grip to be taken;
(c) as in 2(b) but add a 'looped' shot in front of the face to be 'dabbed' with frying-pan grip.

HITTING ACTION

This should always be a free, throwing action. Overhead shots are played as a cricketer throws from the boundary; drives are played as a cricketer throws in from cover-point or near the wicket, or as a stone is skimmed across water; lobs and high serves are played as a cricketer throws in underhand from a distance; and the low serve is like the gentle lobbing of a ball to a child.

THE WRIST

The wrist, like a universal joint, can be turned to right or left, or be bent backwards or forwards. By turning the palm, wrist and forearm to the right for overhead shots and to the left for underhand shots, the racquet face is brought square to the shuttle, or at such an angle as to be able to deflect the shuttle deceptively in any direction. It should also be cocked or bent back before every shot. When the wrist is strongly uncocked, some 2ft before impact, the speed of wrist movement is added to the speed of arm movement (cf. the swift acceleration of the 'Whip' at a fun fair). It is this action that adds real sting to a shot. It must be precisely timed: if the wrist is uncocked too soon, no power is added at impact; if it is uncocked too late, maximum power is never generated. Care must be taken that the action is not overdone : that the racquet face is not 'snatched' so quickly across the shuttle that it is mishit (Plates 4a, 4b and 5).

PRACTICES

1. Off court, play strokes with slow arm action but try to get the loudest 'swish' by use of wrist.

2. On court, as above, but try to get maximum power with minimum arm swing.

THE SWING

BACKSWING

The essence of power-throwing is the longest possible backswing. It is, therefore, essential to start the backswing early (before the shuttle crosses the net). The racquet head must be swept back firmly, and deliberately. By bending the elbow, it is brought roughly between the shoulder-blades. The wrist is cocked back at the same time (Plates 6, 7, 8, 17, 35 and 42).

FORWARD SWING

In this the action speeds up, smoothly and rhythmically. The heel of the hand leads, the arm is snapped straight and the wrist is strongly uncocked; the arm is straight at impact. In overhead and underarm strokes, body and arm are close and in line to ensure power and control. Body weight now swings forward.

The left arm and hand can also play a part. By moving in a direction opposite to that of the backswing or forward swing, they act as a counterbalance. Some players, in overhead shots, use the hand as a sighting guide to the shuttle. In backhand strokes, it may be used to pull the racquet across and back in a full backswing (Plates 9, 11 and 26).

POINT OF IMPACT AND FOLLOW-THROUGH

Roughly speaking, the point of impact for all shots except the defensive clear and floating drop, is just ahead of the front foot. The player should always try to hit into and through the shuttle. The racquet face is kept as square to the base of the shuttle as angling permits, to keep down mishits. The shuttle should be cut only for deliberate deception as to speed, in a smash or drop-shot; otherwise loss of power or a mishit will result. (Plates 9, 18, 20, 22 and 27).

In the follow-through, the racquet head continues thus along the shuttle's line of flight as long as possible if the player leans into the stroke. Remember the shuttle remains on the strings at impact for a fraction of a second. Any 'snatching' with the racquet head will therefore cause a mishit. For accuracy the racquet head is aimed at the desired target area. A long follow-through is the least tiring way of decelerating a fast-moving arm. Over-riding this, however, will often be the need to bring the racquet rapidly back into the 'ready' position, in front of the stomach (Plates 11, 19, 22, 23, 25, 28 and 44).

THE BODY

To ensure full power and control of shots, the body must be correctly used. Body weight should always be transferred to the back foot during the backswing. With the forward swing, the weight is swayed forward on to the front foot so the body is nearly square to the net. In power-shots this is a strong movement that adds speed to the shuttle. In more delicate shots a gentle sway is just as essential; for perfect control, body and arm must be working together in line. One of the commonest causes of mishits is that the player leans away from, and not into, the shuttle at impact; consequently the racquet is pulled away from the shuttle and a mishit results.

Body weight leaning into the shot also helps the start of a quick recovery in overhead and side-arm strokes (Plates 11, 18, 34).

FOOTWORK

Fluent strokes without fluent movement will avail a player little! Footwork is the very mainspring of badminton. It gives a player the following advantages:

1. If the shuttle is reached while it is still above tape height an outright winner can be scored. A split second later the chance is lost (Plate 40).

2. Opponent has less time to regain his base and prepare stroke.

3. A wider variety of shots can be played.

4. Quick recovery narrows gaps and ensures returns (Plate 16).

5. More consistent and accurate shots will be played if the striker is well-balanced and momentarily static as he plays the shot rather than if he is still lumbering into position. Such early, fluent movement is based on a number of points, mental and physical, as follows.

MENTAL APPROACH

QUICK PERCEPTION

This is dealt with fully under 'Eye' (p. 50). The player must be trained to pick up and appreciate the line of flight of the shuttle almost as it is hit. Nerve impulses from brain to muscle are roughly constant for all players but 'grooving' of a shot does reduce the intervals between impulses, reducing reaction time (Plate 15).

ANTICIPATION

With experience, wise anticipation will allow still earlier movement. All players must learn not only what is the orthodox or likely reply to a shot but more particularly what are their opponents' favourite shots from certain parts of the court and their limitations under pressure (e.g. the overplayed cross-court drops, or the backhand drop because the clear is weak). Then the player can position himself a foot or so nearer the anticipated target or on rare (but highly pleasurable) occasions move direct to that spot, as the shuttle is hit.

KILLER INSTINCT

Only this will constantly spur a player always to be moving to the shuttle, never waiting for it to come to him. He must seek to reach the shuttle ever earlier, to hammer it down, to be rapacious for winners (Plate 11).

PHYSICAL APPROACH

This mental approach must work hand-in-hand with physical form.

FITNESS

Its vital importance and the means of achieving it are fully dealt with in Chapter 13.

POSITION OF READINESS

This is the springboard of all movement. Players should have their weight forward, be on the balls of their feet, with knees slightly bent. Feet may be moving very slightly, like a boxer's, and should be shoulder width apart. If movement forward or backward is anticipated, the left foot is a little ahead of the right; if movement sideways, the feet are roughly parallel. The racquet is held across the stomach to protect that vulnerable

49

target, and to be equidistant for backhand and forehand shots (Plates 15 and 39).

Players must be imbued with a sense of urgency, especially in moving backwards; it is a false economy to save a little energy by sluggishness. Once the shuttle is behind a player, both the stroke itself and recovery become more difficult. After forward swing and follow-through, feet must be instantly forced into recovery towards base or the next shot; there can be no waiting to admire the stroke. Ideally, the striker is well poised on base before his opponent again hits the shuttle. It is so easy to turn a shuttle away from a player still moving fast! (Plate 15).

ACTUAL MOVEMENT
Movement forward is invariably by running; movement backward either by running or by chasséing (skipping). Movement sideways is generally by one or two chassés followed by a long stride across after pivoting on the outer foot; sometimes, when moving rapidly across the full width of the court, it is by running. In all cases the player generally starts with short steps for acceleration, and finishes with a longer stride for positioning and stopping (Figs. 8 and 9; Plates 16 and 43).

Although chasséing ensures the player is always correctly poised for overhead shots, while running may need an adjusted step, there is little to choose between them. In both cases, steps should be light, flowing and floor-skimming. Players should experiment to see which method suits them best.

STOPPING
It is equally important that a player should be able to stop quickly and on balance. This can be achieved by a final longer stride with knees bent and the centre of gravity over the foot-base when stopping. One extra step after hitting a shot means *two* steps wasted. Under- and side-arm strokes should be played at as full a stretch as is consistent with balance and recovery. The body then is kept as near base as possible and the shuttle is neither over-run, nor hit with a cramped action.

Practice: see under Agility and Pressure Training for Shuttle and Maze runs (pp. 135–137) and Two v One practices (pp. 132–133).

EYE

Correct use of the eye is essential not only for clean striking of

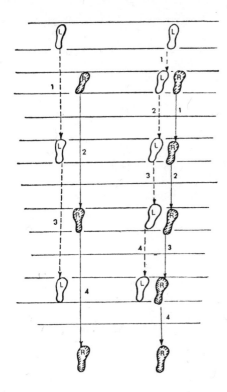

A   B

Fig. 8. Movement backwards: A. Running. B. *Chasséing*.

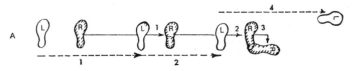

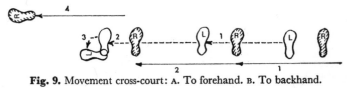

Fig. 9. Movement cross-court: A. To forehand. B. To backhand.

the shuttle but also for quick movement and shrewd placement.

HITTING THE SHUTTLE

Every endeavour should be made to watch the shuttle on to the very strings. This is easily done with slower shots but it is obviously extremely difficult with faster shots. Because of the curving trajectory of the former it is essential to see them actually on to the strings. It is all too easy to take one's eye off the shuttle in the last 18 inches or so before impact. This is mainly caused by lack of concentration or over-confidence. It results in missing the shuttle altogether, in snatching desperately at it, or in mishitting. Another reason, particularly when playing under pressure and threatened at the net, is to see how the shuttle is being dealt with. It is essential to keep the head down and still for a fraction of a second before looking up for the return (Plates 9, 15, 26 and 44).

EARLY MOVEMENT

This stems from keen and intelligent watching of the opponent's racquet at impact. If the angle of the racquet face and its speed can be assessed, the shot can be anticipated or the flight of the shuttle discerned very shortly after the shuttle is hit. In this way a second is saved on the player who is not able to pick up the line of flight until the shuttle is on his side of the net. Observe, too, the position of the opponent's body and feet, and backswing, which may betray the shot to come.

It is also essential to use peripheral vision to the full. While the main focus of the eye is always kept on the shuttle, the movement of opponents can still be observed by the periphery of the eye. Thus, almost subconsciously, the striker sees just before he hits the shuttle where best to place it : into a gap or to the weaker player.

PRACTICES

1. Simple rallies (e.g. clears) growing ever longer, watching shuttle from racquet to racquet.

2. Single with coach in which student concentrates on early spotting of shuttle's trajectory in smash, drop or clear.

3. Single, with coach, in which player seeks always to get behind overhead returns and not merely keep pace with them.

4. As in (3) but player also concentrating on flowing into instant movement from his stroke so that he is well balanced on base before his opponent again strikes the shuttle.

52

7

STROKE PRODUCTION
AND CORRECTION

The following notes should be read in conjunction with Chapter 6 'Basic Techniques'. They give sufficient details of stroke production and correction, and of their tactical application, to enable the coach to have ample material for a lesson (Fig. 10).

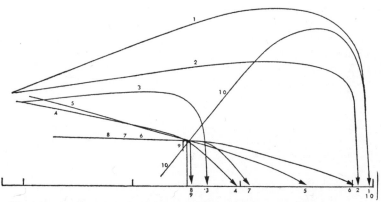

Fig. 10. Trajectories: (1) Defensive clear. (2) Attacking clear. (3) Floating drop. (4) Fast drop. (5) Smash. (6) Drive. (7) Half-court push. (8) Side-arm drop shot. (9) Net shot. (10) Lob.

CLEARS

THE DEFENSIVE CLEAR

This basic overhead stroke is played with a free throwing action. It is a defensive one by which the shuttle is hit high and deep from one base line to the other.

BASIC USE : In singles, it is much used as a means of forcing a single opponent so far back that he cannot attack strongly.

53

In doubles, it is used much more rarely, often as an expedient to recover when off balance or if no better shot can be played. In mixed it is used still more rarely because the man has to defend the whole width of the court.

GRIP : Basic.

FEET : 45° to shuttle's line of flight; left in front of right so that left shoulder is pointing to net.

BACKSWING : Either by (a) bringing racquet up, out, and round shoulder, or up and over shoulder, or (b) swinging racquet down and back so that the 'head' is brought roughly between the shoulderblades; the elbow is up, the arm well bent, and the wrist cocked back (Plates 6 and 7).

FORWARD SWING : With the heel of the hand leading, the arm is snapped straight, the wrist is uncocked and body weight swings forward (Plate 8).

IMPACT : Just above right shoulder, when racquet head is at 45°, to give maximum height and length.

FOLLOW-THROUGH : To about waist height.

ERROR : (1) Lacks power so poor length and easily killed.

CORRECTION : (a) Start backswing earlier so that there is time for arm to be straight, not bent, at impact (help by calling 'Back!' and 'Up!' at appropriate moments). Throw – don't 'dab' or 'bowl'.

(b) See that grip and stance are correct.

(c) Swing arm faster, bringing in wrist and finger snap strongly at correct point. (It is better to swing and miss rather than just dab.)

(d) Ensure that racquet head is dropped right between shoulderblades at end of backswing, that arm is kept close to head in forward swing, and that body leans strongly into shot.

ERROR : (2) Shuttle hit too low, and therefore intercepted.

CORRECTION : Play shuttle later, just behind head, with straight arm, and racquet head at 45°.

ERROR : (3) Shuttle hit too high, and therefore often short.

CORRECTION : Speed up footwork so that shuttle is struck correctly, and not behind the body.

ERROR : (4) Mishitting or cutting shuttle.

CORRECTION : Check grip; keep racquet face square to shuttle at impact; hit 'into' and 'through' shuttle, not across it with exaggerated wrist action.

ERROR : (5) Missing shuttle.

CORRECTION : Watch shuttle on to racquet; start backswing early; be relaxed.

54

THE ATTACKING CLEAR

This is an attacking shot played from near the base line. The shuttle is hit hard but with only just sufficient elevation to avoid interception.

BASIC USE : It is used in all types of games as an occasional unexpected alternative to defensive clear, drop or smash, when the opponent is too far forward from his central base but the striker is well positioned.

HOW PLAYED : Exactly as the defensive clear except that the point of impact is some 12 inches farther forward with the racquet head almost at right angles to the floor.

ERROR : (1) Shuttle hit too high so giving opponent time for recovery.

CORRECTION : Take shuttle earlier, so that at impact racquet face is almost vertical to floor.

Errors (1), (3), (4) and (5) in Defensive Clear also apply.

THE ROUND-ARM CLEAR

This is a shot to be played only in an emergency when the shuttle is so far behind the striker that a normal clear is impracticable. The swing is basically a bowling action ending in a strong whipped action of forearm and wrist just before impact. (A weak but surprise smash can be played in the same way.)

THE DROP SHOT

THE SLOW OR FLOATING DROP SHOT

This is a gently hit but attacking shot played from behind the doubles back service line so that it lands as near the net as possible (1-4ft).

BASIC USE : In men's and ladies' doubles and singles as an alternative to a defensive clear :

(a) To force a weak defensive lob or a net shot.

(b) To create an opening by moving opponents out of position.

HOW PLAYED : For deception, just like the defensive clear until late in the . . .

FORWARD SWING : Arm swing is then greatly slowed down; or, alternatively, as in other slowed-down deception shots, stopped sharply at impact.

IMPACT : Above right shoulder when the racquet face is almost vertical to the ground so that the shuttle is hit flat or slightly upwards.

FOLLOW-THROUGH : Short and firm.

ERROR : (1) Shuttle hit too high; therefore easily intercepted at net.

CORRECTION : Take shuttle earlier and do not give it too much 'air'.

ERROR : (2) No deception because shuttle, allowed to fall too low, is hit with a dabbing action.

CORRECTION : Player clears with full, straight-arm action, then gradually changes strength of stroke and point of impact to those mentioned above.

ERROR : (3) Shuttle falls into or short of net.

CORRECTION : Hit shuttle slightly more upwards; make follow-through more positive.

THE FAST DROP SHOT

This is a stroke of medium strength played from the back doubles service line or behind. It travels fairly fast and steeply to skim the tape and to land on, or slightly behind, the front service line.

BASIC USE : It is used largely by the man in mixed when he is too deep in court to play a smash. Its aim is either (a) to draw the opposing man up court or (b) to run the opposing lady to and fro across court by speed of shot and deception, and to force her to play an uncontrolled shot which can be still more strongly attacked.

HOW PLAYED : Like the smash (q.v.) except that late in the forward swing, speed is reduced by about half.

ERROR : (1) Shuttle hit into net.

CORRECTION : Take shuttle slightly less far forward.

ERROR : (2) No deception.

CORRECTION : Turn wrist just before impact to give change of direction; make stroke look like a smash until last second.

Errors (1a), (1b) and (1d) and (5) of Defensive Clear also apply.

THE SMASH

THE BASIC SMASH

This is the power stroke that so satisfyingly ends rallies and wins points. It is played from any part of the court forward of the back doubles service line. It is hit downwards as hard and as steeply as possible to beat the opponent by sheer speed and to land about 6-8ft behind the front service line (Plates 6-9).

BASIC USE : It is used in all types of game to end a rally or to make an opening. It should be hit (a) into a gap or (b) into the right side of the body. Steepness, consistency, placement and power are vital qualities.

HOW PLAYED : Like the defensive clear up to late in the ...

FORWARD SWING : The wrist is then fully uncocked to bring the racquet face over the shuttle at ...

IMPACT : This is 12-18in ahead of the right shoulder.

FOLLOW-THROUGH : Sweeps down and past legs.

ERROR : (1) Shuttle hit flat and therefore easily counter-attacked.

CORRECTION : Speed up footwork and swing so that shuttle is taken earlier in front of head; uncock wrist more strongly.

Make student walk into shuttle and try to hit it *into* the net.

ERROR : (2) Mishitting.

CORRECTION : Avoid tenseness and over-hitting, and 'snatching' with wrist; make swing easy and relaxed. Keep eye on shuttle and not on target.

Errors (1), (4) and (5) of Defensive Clear also apply here.

ROUND-THE-HEAD SMASH

This attacking shot, a cross between a drive and a smash, is played when the shuttle is a little above head height and just on the backhand (Plates 13 and 14).

BASIC USE : It is often used to kill drive serves aimed at the backhand and to seize a fleeting opening in mixed. Care must be taken to hit slightly downwards, to maintain balance, and not to overplay cross-court shots.

GRIP : Basic.

FEET : Slightly more than shoulder width apart; left foot only a little in advance of right, and both at right-angles to the net.

BACKSWING : Racquet is swept quickly up, back and behind the head; arm is bent and wrist cocked back.

FORWARD SWING : Bent arm sweeps across top of the head; strong forearm and wrist action are used; body is arched and leaning sideways with weight on left foot.

IMPACT : Over or outside left shoulder, a little above head.

FOLLOW-THROUGH : Short for the straight shot but across the body for the cross-court shot.

ERROR : (1) Dabbing action because arm is brought up late and in front of face.

57

CORRECTION: Start swing earlier and 'feel the arm brush across the top of the head'.

OVERHEAD BACKHAND STROKES

As with overhead forehand strokes, these consist of the clear (defensive and attacking), the drop shot (slow and fast), and the smash. Since they are often regarded as an Achilles' heel to be attacked mercilessly, they must be strengthened by regular practice. While no shot should be played backhanded that can be played more effectively forehanded, without leaving the striker off balance or out of position, players must be discouraged from coddling their backhand by trying to run round it (Plates 17, 18, 19 and 20).

BASIC USE: As for similar forehand strokes except that since the backhand smash is weaker than the forehand one it should be used from several feet farther forward.

GRIP: Basic or backhand.

FEET: Point out to the back corner of the court at about 45° with right foot in front of left so that back of right shoulder is to the net.

BACKSWING: As striker turns to back of court, racquet head is dropped thigh-high in front of body; knees and back are slightly bent; elbow is bent and pointing upwards into shuttle; wrist is cocked.

FORWARD SWING: Body and shoulders turn into shot as elbow leads before arm snaps straight and wrist strongly uncocks; legs straighten and body arches like uncoiling spring.

IMPACT: As with forehand strokes.

FOLLOW-THROUGH: Much more restricted than for forehand shots.

ERROR: (1) Lack of power in clear.

CORRECTION: Make backswing longer; speed up sweep of arm; time wrist-snap to split second; take shuttle above head.

Minor errors and corrections are as for the forehand shots already described.

THE DRIVE

THE FOREHAND DRIVE

This crisp shot is played from roughly mid-court near the side lines, and hit fast and flat (Plates 26 and 28).

BASIC USE : It is used, particularly in mixed by the man, as an attacking alternative to the smash, when the shuttle cannot be struck well above the head but has fallen to just above tape height. It should be met early and hit, slightly downwards or flat, straight or cross-court, into a gap or into a badly positioned defender's body. It is dangerous to hit it up, or at an alert defender because of the speed of the subsequent return.

GRIP : Basic.

FEET : Both feet point to the side lines; the left is 12-15 inches in advance of, and slightly nearer the net than, the right foot. To ensure a quick recovery, experienced stroke players often play this shot with the right foot across.

BACKSWING : The racquet head is brought up and back behind the right shoulder so that it is nearly between the shoulder-blades; the arm is bent, the wrist cocked, and the elbow at tape level.

FORWARD SWING : Turning body from the hips to face net, the player flings the racquet forward in a wide arc, straightening the arm and half uncocking the wrist.

IMPACT : Just in front of leading foot at about tape height. For cross-court shot, it is a foot farther forward.

FOLLOW-THROUGH : The player leans into the shot, keeping racquet head square to shuttle as long as possible before sweeping it across the body.

ERROR : (1) Cross-courting too often.

CORRECTION : Play shuttle later : force racquet-head to continue parallel to side-lines.

ERROR : (2) Lacks power.

CORRECTION : Start backswing earlier and make it longer; play shuttle at arm's length and make shot a fling of the whole arm and not just a push of the forearm.

ERROR : (3) Mishitting.

CORRECTION : Lean into shot so keeping racquet face square to shuttle as long as possible.

ERROR : (4) Shuttle hit out over side line.

CORRECTION : Check grip; start backswing earlier so shuttle is met in front of, not behind, leading foot.

THE BACKHAND DRIVE

GRIP : Backhand (Plate 2b).

FEET : Both feet pointing to side lines with right foot 12-18 inches ahead of, and rather nearer the net than, the left foot.

BACKSWING: Racquet head swung back roughly between shoulderblades; arm is bent and wrist cocked.

FORWARD SWING: With shoulder as pivot, racquet is flung in wide arc, elbow pointing to shuttle arm straightening and wrist uncocking.

IMPACT: Tape high, just in front of right foot (Plate 27).

FOLLOW-THROUGH: As for forehand drive.

Errors (1), (2) and (3) for Forehand Drive apply here also.

THE LOFTED DRIVE (BACKHAND)

This hybrid, half-drive, half-lob, is known to some as the 'Danish Wipe' because it is used largely by Danish ladies and it is indeed a wipe. It is hit hard and high, on a rising trajectory, from deep in the backhand corner to the opposite base line.

BASIC USE: It is used as an alternative to overhead backhand shots when these are not strong. It has the disadvantages that (a) it is tiring; (b) the shuttle is hit upwards and (c) it gives opponents longer to regain position, but it enables a good length to be hit and can take players by surprise.

HOW PLAYED: Like the backhand drive except that body twists round more, and in the forward swing, the elbow is swept slightly down and the racquet face is brought under the shuttle and up, angled at $45°$. The follow-through is forward of and above the right shoulder.

THE HALF-COURT PUSH AND DROP SHOT

These probing shots are hit flat from the side lines, from 2-8ft behind the front service line, to a point 2-3ft behind the service line or to the net.

BASIC USE: They are used both in mixed and in men's and ladies' doubles when the opposing pair is playing back and front. The half-court shot should be just fast enough to pass the net player and yet not quite reach the back player, thus drawing them together and opening up the whole court. The drop shot is played to a slow net player and can be interspersed with similar cross-court shots. To make them effective, these shots must both be played exactly like the drive. The wrist should be kept back until the last second so that the threat of a drive or a cross-court shot is held.

HOW PLAYED: Just like the drive, except that the arm action is slowed down just before impact. Particularly with drop shots, the racquet face should be angled slightly more upwards to overcome gravitational pull so that shuttle is not hit into net. Errors (3) and (4) of the Drive apply here also.

THE NET SHOTS

These strokes (basic, stab, hair-pin, dab, brush and dead racquet), as their name implies, are shots played from very near and just over the net. They are played with either (a) a caressing delicacy, upwards, to creep just over the tape or (b) with crispness, downwards, as steeply as possible.

BASIC USE: Upward net shots are a good alternative to a lob, for, if accurately played, it is the opponent who is forced into error or has to lift the shuttle. Downward net shots seek to finish off a rally with an outright winner.
NB. Net player must keep racquet up at tape height throughout rally.

THE UPWARD NET SHOTS

GRIP: Basic.
FEET: Roughly the same as for drives but immaterial provided body can lean into strokes.
BACKSWING, FORWARD SWING, IMPACT, FOLLOW-THROUGH: With arm slightly bent, and wrist uncocking very slightly, the shuttle is met as near tape as possible, stroked, and firmly followed through. The whole is a perfect miniature stroke in a compass of about 9 inches (Plates 33, 34 and 41).
ERROR: (1) Shuttle taken too low.
CORRECTION: By keeping on balls of feet and with racquet constantly at tape height, go in to meet shuttle early.
ERROR: (2) Wild stabbing at shuttle.
CORRECTION: Relax, play stroke more slowly; merely stroke shuttle or just lean into the shot.
ERROR: (3) Hit too high.
CORRECTION: Uncock wrist only very slightly, using relaxed but firm basic finger grip.
ERROR: (4) Shuttle 'fluffed' on racquet or hit into net.
CORRECTION: Play firmly; sway body into stroke; watch shuttle on to strings; follow through – and TAKE CARE!

THE STAB

This is used only when the shuttle is no more than 6 inches

below tape height. The racquet head is stabbed or thrust horizontally under the shuttle. This gives the advantage that the shuttle turns fairly fast and often goes over the net feathers first. It is difficult to control, but forces the receiver to let the shuttle drop a little or risk a mishit.

THE HAIR-PIN

In this stroke the shuttle is taken well below tape height and hit almost vertically upwards to rise some 6 inches above the tape before dropping, again almost vertically, very near the net. This makes a deep lob almost an impossibility. It is played, mainly in singles, when the opponent is too deep in court to attack it.

THE DOWNWARD NET SHOTS
THE DAB

GRIP : Basic or frying-pan; loosely in backswing but tightly at impact.
FEET : Immaterial provided body leans into shot.
BACKSWING : Directly back for no more than a foot.
FORWARD SWING : The bent forearm is pushed slightly forward and the wrist uncocked to dab the shuttle crisply down.
IMPACT : Just in front of body at tape height (Plate 32).
FOLLOW-THROUGH : Definite but very short so that net is not hit. The whole stroke is played in a compass of about 18 inches.
ERROR : (1) Shuttle hit out.
CORRECTION : Use more wrist so shuttle is hit down and not flat. Remember there is only 22 feet of court ahead.
ERROR : (2) Hit into net.
CORRECTION : Keep racquet head up between rallies; restrict backswing; take early; and lean into shot.

THE BRUSH

This is a variant of the dab played while the shuttle is so near the tape, or even fractionally below it, that a dab would result in the racquet hitting the net. The striker gets well down to this stroke. He brushes his racquet, angled slightly upwards, with a rotary and slightly forward movement, across the base of the shuttle. The stroke is deceptive in that the shuttle appears to be hit hard to one side of the court whereas it drops straight and quite close to the net (Plate 40).

THE DEAD RACQUET SHOT

This may be played just above tape height or with arm fully upstretched. At impact, the racquet, held in a loose finger grip, is allowed to give slightly. As a result, the shuttle drops almost vertically from the racquet face very close to the net, with the pace taken from it.

THE SERVES

THE LOW SERVE

This beautifully delicate and accurate stroke should be so hit that it literally skims the tape and drops some 6 inches behind the opposite short service line. Deceptively simple, it nevertheless needs constant practice. Remember that when the shuttle is hit, it must be below waist height and that no part of the racquet head must be above any part of the hand (Law 14), so keep the racquet almost vertical (Fig. 12 and Plate 21).

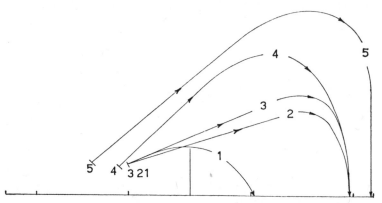

Fig. 11. Trajectories of serves: 1. Low; 2. Drive; 3. Flick; 4. High; 5. Very high (singles).

BASIC USE : It is the standard doubles service, used most of the time. If accurately played, it forces the opponents on to the defensive by lifting the shuttle to the server, who has now moved into the net, or to his partner at the back of the court. It is generally served to the centre of the T-junction so that any return, at least theoretically, passes within the reach of server or partner. It is occasionally varied, at the risk of the angle being opened, by being hit to the outside corners.

GRIP: Basic; this may be shortened, however, by 6 inches for more control.

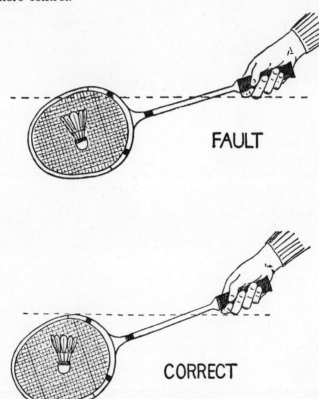

Fig. 12. Correct and fault services (*reproduced by courtesy of BA of E*).

SHUTTLE: Held by feathers between thumb and forefinger, at about shoulder height, to drop just by leading foot.

FEET: Left foot a little in advance of right at 45° to the net. (As power is not needed, some players prefer right foot forward.)

BACKSWING: Weight sways on to rear foot as racquet head is brought back to right of, and about a foot behind, right thigh; elbow bent and close to body; wrist cocked fully back.

FORWARD SWING: As shuttle is released, weight sways forward, and the whole arm (elbow still bent and wrist still cocked)

64

MOVEMENT

15 Absolutely alert, Margaret Allen is just moving swiftly and smoothly away from position of readiness

16 Superb action: Paul Whetnall shows how fitness, determination and concentration enable him to make amazing recoveries from any corner of the court

16

17

18

19

17 Margaret Allen is moving neatly across to the deep backhand corner; racquet head dropping, elbow coming up, left foot coming across, back of shoulder to net

18 Just after impact; arm and wrist snapped straight; body swung into shot

19 Follow-through: limited of necessity but showing unusually strong wrist flick; eyes still on point of impact

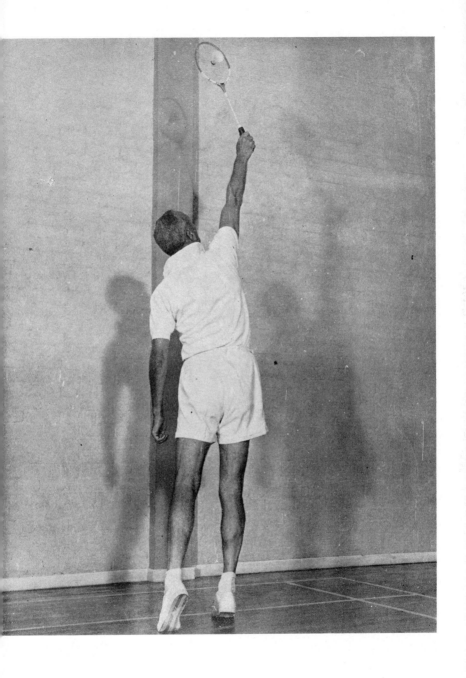

20 Pat Davis shows how a right-hander plays the stroke; arm straight and nearly vertical; wrist uncocking strongly, back of right shoulder to net; shuttle taken at full stretch

21

22

23

LOW SERVE
21 Peter Roper (Suffolk County Coach)
demonstrates the compact low serve: just
before impact; weight on left foot; arm well
bent to take shuttle high, wrist fully cocked
back; left foot forward but body turning
square to net; shuttle released from finger
grip
22 Just after impact: wrist still cocked; head
still down as racquet head is aimed at target
area
23 Tyna Barinaga sends shuttle skimming over
the tape with a longer and freer swing

24   25

BACKHAND SERVE
24 Beginning of forward swing: toeing the line, with weight slightly forward on right foot, Ray, with backhand grip and arm well bent, swings racquet forward from just behind left thigh, shuttle held low to avoid striking it above waist

25 Fractionally after impact just below waist level: restricted but firm follow-through; head still down

26

27

DRIVES
26 Halfway through forward swing: arm straightening but wrist still cocked

27 Backhand at impact: right foot across; arm straight and wrist uncocked; shuttle taken just in front of body

28 Paul Whetnall with right foot across and arm straight has just driven shuttle at shoulder height down side line; he is well balanced for quick recovery

29

DEFENCE

29 The Author shows the orthodox flat push return: right foot across; arm bent; wrist firm; eyes watching the shuttle; grim concentration; taken early in front of the vulnerable right side

Ray Sharp demonstrates two unorthodox replies for emergency use only that have a shattering moral effect on the opposition

30 Between the legs: used when the racquet is to right of body and a shot has been played straight into it

31 Round the back: no time to bring the racquet across in front of the body so Ray brings it behind

30

31

swings forward with it in a pendulum-like action (Plate 21).
IMPACT : Just by toe of leading foot (Plate 22).
FOLLOW-THROUGH : Firmly, on target, to about waist height (Plate 23).

Height of tape and opponent's position should be observed before each serve and distance to target area assessed. The server should be relaxed and deliberate; the stroke, a firm caress. Wrist, and therefore racquet head, must be kept cocked back throughout.

ERROR : (1) Shuttle hit into net.
CORRECTION : Look at tape; watch shuttle on to strings and keep head down fractionally after impact; hit shuttle a little earlier and harder; uncock wrist very slightly.
ERROR : (2) Shuttle hit too high.
CORRECTION : Relax; keep wrist cocked right back; keep stance upright; play shuttle a little later.
ERROR : (3) Hit too deep.
CORRECTION : Do not hit hard but rather let gentle arm-swing be generated by forward body-sway.
ERROR : (4) Faulty placement.
CORRECTION : Aim racquet head at target at impact and in follow-through.
ERROR : (5) Shuttle hit short.
CORRECTION : Carefully gauge distance especially cross-court and follow-through firmly.
ERROR : (6) Missing shuttle altogether.
CORRECTION : Let student shorten grip and merely drop shuttle on to racquet held in front of him. Length of backswing and grip are slowly increased. Watch on to strings.

THE FLICK SERVE

This enjoyable deceptive shot looks like the low serve until the last second when, by a flick of the wrist, it is hit just high enough over the receiver to avoid early interception.

BASIC USE : It is used in doubles to either corner as a variant of the low serve when the latter is being punished. Its occasional use and constant threat hold back even the most zealous receiver.
HOW PLAYED : For deception, it is exactly like the low serve until a foot before impact when the wrist is uncocked crisply.

ERROR : (1) No deception.

CORRECTION : Make sure that backswing is no longer, and forward swing is no faster, than that for the low serve.

Uncock wrist at shortest possible distance before impact.

Keep routine exactly the same: i.e. do not take longer or look at back service line instead of tape.

ERROR : (2) Shuttle hit too high, so receiver has time to recover.

CORRECTION : Use rather less wrist.

ERROR : (3) Shuttle hit too short, so easily intercepted.

CORRECTION : Push forward more in follow-through.

ERROR : (4) Shuttle hit too low.

CORRECTION : Use more wrist.

THE DRIVE SERVE

The shuttle is hit flat and fast to skim the net and land near the back doubles service line. It is another surprise alternative to the low serve.

BASIC USE : It is generally aimed at a receiver standing near the front service line, at his backhand, or into a gap if he is badly placed. The server must be ready for an equally quick return.

HOW PLAYED : Exactly like the low serve until just before impact when arm speed is rapidly increased.

ERROR : (1) Lack of deception.

CORRECTION : Do not lengthen backswing or speed up forward swing too early.

ERROR : (2) Shuttle hit too high so easier to attack.

CORRECTION : Keep wrist cocked; hold shuttle about shoulder height.

THE BACKHAND SERVE

This is an increasingly used variant which was introduced by the Malayans. It has these advantages: (a) its very novelty worries opponents; (b) with the white shuttle held in front of a white shirt, it is more difficult to see quickly; (c) it travels an even shorter distance to the receiver.

GRIP : Shortened backhand grip.

FEET : Right foot forward almost on front service line.

SHUTTLE : Held high in front of chest and a little forward of the right foot.

BACKSWING : With elbow raised, racquet is swung back to left side of body beneath outstretched left arm, so that right hand

66

is almost beneath left armpit; arm is bent and wrist cocked (Plate 24).

FORWARD SWING : Forearm pushes racquet forward.

IMPACT : In front of right foot (Plate 25).

NB. It is very easy to fault serve by hitting shuttle at above waist level.

Errors for the Low Serve also apply here.

THE HIGH SERVE

This is hit from the normal base, or a little farther back in court, anything from 18-30ft high.

BASIC USE : It is the staple serve in singles as it drives the receiver so far back in court that few players (Rudi Hartono and Kops excepted?) can smash it effectively. In doubles, where it must be hit 2ft 6in less deep, it is used more sparingly; i.e. (a) to a lady weak overhead; (b) by a pair very strong in defence; (c) to slow the tempo of a game when other serves are being killed.

GRIP : Basic.

FEET : About 45° to centre line.

SHUTTLE : As for low serve but some 6-12 inches farther forward.

BACKSWING : Again as for low serve, but racquet is taken farther back until it is nearly at right-angles to the floor (Plate 35).

FORWARD SWING : Fast downward pendulum sweep with arm nearly straightening and wrist uncocking strongly (Plate 36).

IMPACT : Slightly in front of leading foot (Plate 37).

FOLLOW-THROUGH : Long, with racquet head finishing in front of, and above height of, left shoulder (Plate 38).

ERROR : (1) Lacks length.

CORRECTION : Make full swing of arm and use wrist more strongly.

ERROR : (2) Lacks height.

CORRECTION : Hit crisply, using wrist more strongly.

THE LOBS (OR UNDERARM CLEARS)

THE FOREHAND LOB

This is an underhand, basically defensive stroke, by which the shuttle is hit high and deep, from near the floor between the net and front service line to the base line. It is the reply to a net shot or a drop shot.

BASIC USE: It is used as a means of recovery when, in singles or in men's and ladies' doubles, a player can only just reach one of the above shots. It is generally hit high to give the striker time to regain his base, and deep, to blunt the opponents' attack. By judicious lessening of height, it can be made into an attacking shot when a singles opponent has been drawn right up to the net, or when a doubles player is hurried from side to side of the court.

GRIP: Basic.

FEET: A lunge position with left foot about 24 inches ahead of the right foot and pointing to the shuttle. The left knee is well bent and the right leg outstretched with toes only on the floor. (Some players prefer putting the right foot to the shuttle to keep nearer base and to gain reach.)

BACKSWING: Racquet drawn down and back to right side and rear of body, arm bent, wrist cocked, and racquet head at about shoulder height.

FORWARD SWING: Racquet head swept down and forward with heel of hand leading, as arm nearly straightens and wrist uncocks strongly about 18 inches before impact.

IMPACT: Just beside and forward of leading foot (Plate 45).

FOLLOW-THROUGH: To above head height. (Head is kept down momentarily.)

In all, this stroke is very like the high serve played at full stretch. Quick recovery is effected by a strong thrust of the bent, front leg.

ERROR: (1) Stroke cramped so lacking power and drawing striker too far from base.

CORRECTION: Make last stride a long one and 'throw' racquet fluently.

ERROR: (2) Lack of height; so little time to regain base safely.

CORRECTION: Use more wrist.

ERROR: (3) Lack of length; so vulnerable to smash.

CORRECTION: Sweep racquet forward as well as upwards.

ERROR: (4) Shuttle mishit.

CORRECTION: Keep eyes on shuttle and head down after impact (cf. golf drive).

THE BACKHAND LOB

GRIP: Backhand.

68

FEET : As above, but right foot points to shuttle.
BACKSWING : Racquet head dropped down and drawn back and up to left side of body above shoulder height; arm is bent and wrist cocked.
FORWARD SWING : With elbow pointing into shuttle, arm straightens and wrist fully uncocks.
IMPACT : Just inside and in front of right foot.
FOLLOW-THROUGH : Firmly forwards and upwards to above shoulder height.

Errors are the same as for the Forehand Lob.

RETURN OF SERVE

These are as varied as they are vital if the receiver is to gain the ascendancy from the outset. Low serves should be taken as near the tape as possible; flick and high serves must obviously be dealt with from deeper in court. They can be played to a wide variety of target areas, to be observed as the receiver takes up his stance.

BASIC USE : This is to score an outright winner or so to place the shuttle that opponents must lift it defensively.
GRIP : Basic or frying-pan.
STANCE : The receiver positions himself as near the front service line as he can while still being able to get back to attack a flick serve. In the right court, he stands about 2ft from the centre line, and in the left court, he will be some 3-4ft from it. The left foot is about 18 inches in front of the right; the knees are bent, and the weight is on the balls of the feet as the receiver crouches forward with the racquet held near the head at tape height. The whole body is dynamically tensed as though for a sprint start. He must constantly seek to stand nearer and nearer the front service line (Plate 39).

THE RETURNS OF LOW SERVE

All these returns are slight variations of basic strokes already described. In each case, however, receiver must try to move to the shuttle as soon as it leaves the server's racquet. (Fig. 18).

Receivers who reach the shuttle only when it is below tape height must play one of these shots:

69

THE LOB
This immediately sacrifices the attack unless it is played deceptively or hit deep to a weak backhand.

THE UPWARD NET SHOT
This is a much better alternative because if played accurately to the corners it will force a lifted shot in return (Plate 41).

Faster movers who meet the shuttle at tape height or above will be able to play these shots:

THE BRUSH
This can be most effectively used to place the shuttle just 'through' a server if he has been intimidated by the apparently strong action (Plate 40).

THE DAB
This can be used to place the shuttle (a) to the corners of the net; (b) half-court; (c) deep to the corners; (d) into the server's partner's chest or (e) crisply down for a winner.

THE RETURNS OF HIGH SERVE

RETURN OF FLICK SERVES
If well on balance and shuttle in front of head, smash. If slightly off balance and shuttle a little behind head, drop. If right off balance and shuttle well behind head, clear.

RETURN OF DRIVE SERVES
If seen early, smash round-the-head. If seen late, play a drop shot by 'blocking' the shuttle, i.e. merely placing the racquet firmly in the shuttle's line of flight.

RETURN OF HIGH SERVES
In doubles, almost invariably smash; in singles, generally use the clear or the drop.

THE RETURNS OF SMASH

The following strokes can all be used as a final defence against the smash, the opponents' most lethal weapon: (a) the lob; (b) the drop shot; (c) the push; (d) the drive; (e) the dab. The immediate aim of each stroke is to wrest the attack from the opponents: to turn defence into offence. This will be better

70

achieved if the striker, whenever possible, moves in from his mid-court base to meet the shuttle earlier. Thus quick, flat shots give his opponents less time in which to recover (Fig. 13).

THE LOB

This is played like the basic lob but not at full stretch. A shorter backswing may be compensated for by a stronger wrist action. The follow-through is more restricted. It is the least effective return as it leaves the attacker still attacking and hopes to gain a point only through his error. To help in this, the lobs should be kept fairly low and hit from side to side of the court.

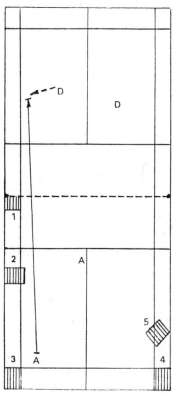

Fig. 13. Placements of return of smash: 1. Drop shot; 2. Half-court push; 3 and 4. Lobs; 5. Drive.

THE PUSH DROP SHOT

This is played as on p. 60 except that the grip should be relaxed slightly to take the pace out of the opponent's smash.

71

It should be used only against a slow net player or one who has dropped back to try and cut off drives.

THE PUSH HALF-COURT
This also is played as on p. 60. Taken early and played down either side line, it can force a lifted return or open up the court (Plates 29, 30 and 31).

THE DRIVE
Played as described on p. 59, it is, for those with a good eye, the best means of seizing the attack. The shuttle should be driven into the smasher's body or into a gap.

THE DAB
Those with a still better eye may (particularly against a flat smasher) move well into the net and play the stroke described on p. 62. If the striker is tall, it pays to bend the knees so that the eyes are just above tape level. Then, with virtually no backswing, the shuttle is dabbed down for a winner (Plate 51).

ERROR : (1) Shuttle missed.
CORRECTION : Watch shuttle from racquet to racquet; use limited backswing; keep eyes down at impact.
ERROR : (2) Shuttle mishit.
CORRECTION : Don't 'snatch' at shuttle belatedly by uncocking wrist too strongly; lean into shot.
ERROR : (3) Shuttle easily intercepted.
CORRECTION : Use varied returns.
ERROR : (4) Hit in body.
CORRECTION : Keep feet mobile and racquet across body.

MOST COMMON FAULTS: THEIR CAUSE AND CORRECTIONS

The correction is generally a verbal reminder reinforced by a demonstration, followed by shadowing and a simple stroke production exercise in which the particular point is stressed. Remedies (numbered) are suggested only when not obvious.

SLUGGISH FOOTWORK

1. Bouncing and skipping exercises on toes. 2. Running backwards. 3. Shuttle runs (all to music). 4. Shadowing stroke and footwork. 5. Shuttle hand fed gradually farther and farther

from striker. 6. Realization of likely return. 7. Watching shuttle off racquet.

MISSING SHUTTLE

Drawing away from shuttle at impact. Not keeping eye on shuttle: 1. Rallies of simple stroke watching shuttle on to racquet. 2. Look for big mark put on base of shuttle.

MISHITTING SHUTTLE

Leaning away from shuttle. Not watching shuttle right on to strings. Hurried wristy 'snatching' at shuttle. Looking up just before impact to see where shuttle is going: 1. 'Head down!' Uncocking wrist too fully and sharply at impact.

LACK OF RACQUET MANOEUVRABILITY

Not initially holding racquet up and across body. Not swinging racquet while moving to shot. Not bringing racquet back to 'ready' immediately after stroke: 1. 'Back – back!'

LACK OF ACCURACY AND CONTROL

Taking shuttle too early or late: 1. Improve footwork. 2. Show point of impact. Not leaning body into shot. Not aiming racquet head at target before and after impact: 1. Target practice. Weak follow-through. Lack of concentration.

LACK OF POWER

Grip too tight or too loose or frying-pan: 1. Grip practices. 2. Check in mid-rally.

Wrist used too early or too late or not at all: 1. Shadowing. 2. Practice exercises. 3. Hitting against wall. 4. Listen for swish. 5. Strengthening exercises (for ladies).

Arm bent, therefore pushing not throwing: 1. Sideways stance. 2. Shadowing with suspended shuttle. 3. *Early,* slow backswing. 4. Start exercises with racquet head between shoulderblades. 5. Call 'Back!'' and 'Up!' for overhead shots. 6. Insist racquet head touches between shoulders. 7. Check feeding.

Body weight not swung into shot: 1. Stand sideways. 2. Move nimbly. 3. Strong backswing and follow-through to ensure weight transfer.

Racquet not tightly strung.

Muscles not developed.

8

TACTICS

HOW THEY CAN BE TAUGHT

Too many coaches talk tactics (sometimes *ad nauseam*); too few teach them. By this I mean approach them logically and inculcate them by demonstration, conditioned games, and practices.

To maintain interest and to build gradually at all levels, tactics may be taught in a variety of ways.

1. All shots should be demonstrated in context, i.e. the cross-court drive is not demonstrated by coach and feed only; four players are in position and the shot played only after 'opponents' have been drawn to side line by straight pushes.

2. As soon as a stroke is first learnt, build it into a simple conditioned game, i.e. one side plays only drops, the other only lobs (see p. 124).

3. Teach a specific tactic in stages: floating drops to the slower opponent to elicit a short lob to be smashed into lobber's body. (a) Practise tight drop and smash into body; (b) Use in conditioned game; (c) Use in friendly game; (d) Use in match.

4. Coach joins in game to create tactical set-up desired.

5. Coach joins in to simulate an opponent's particular skill or weakness.

6. Discussion held round a peg-board court as a 'reasoned' game is played.

7. Stop a game for any tactical error; recreate the set-up, and replay the rally correctly several times.

8. Watch a game or film with students; point out good and bad points and ask leading questions.

MEN'S AND LADIES' DOUBLES
COURT POSITIONS

INITIAL POSITIONS FOR SERVE AND RETURN

At the outset, each pair assumes a back and front attacking position (Plate 46 and Fig. 17).

SERVER (S)

As he has to follow his low serve in to the net, he stands:

1. As near the front service line as he can (1-4ft) in order to be quickly on the T-junction to intercept net returns.

2. As near the centre line as possible in order to be equidistant to such returns to either side.

SERVER'S PARTNER (SP)

He adopts a central position so that he is:

1. Equidistant from the side lines.

2. So placed as to be able to attack equally well both half-court pushes and lobs, and fast push returns of serve left by his partner, yet able to see receiver clearly.

RECEIVER (R)

He stands:

1. As near the front service line as he can while still being able to get back to attack flick serves.

2. In the right court, near the centre line to cover his vulnerable backhand against drive serves.

3. In the left court, centrally, to cover his backhand to some extent but without leaving a gap on his forehand.

RECEIVER'S PARTNER (RP)

He is centrally placed so that he can quickly move to any point in his sector to maintain the attack initiated by his partner.

All players must be so poised and positioned and dynamically alert that they can move in a split second to try and maintain the attack achieved by either server or receiver, or to counter-attack.

SUBSEQUENT POSITIONS FOR ATTACK AND DEFENCE

These initial positions are maintained until one pair is forced on to the defensive. That pair then takes up a sides formation whilst their opponents maintain the attacking back and front positions. Thereafter, each pair moves from one formation to the other as it attacks (hits down) or defends (lifts the shuttle). See Fig. 14 and Plates 47 and 48.

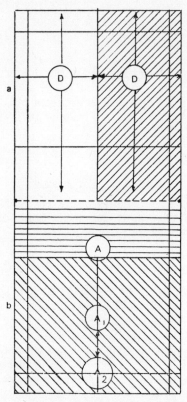

Fig. 14. Attack and defence positions: Attacking back player drives and pushes from A1, but drops back to A2 to deal with clears.

DEFENCE (D)

Each player can move easily to take any shot to his half-court: there are no obvious gaps.

ATTACK (A)

Net player, from A, moves to meet all net shots, pushes and drives. His partner attacks lobs and clears from A_2, moving to A_1 quickly, to deal with flat shots not intercepted by his partner.

76

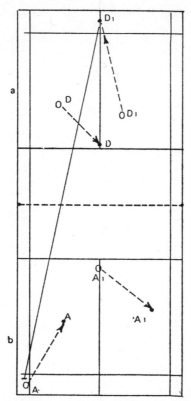

Fig. 15. Transition from attack to defence from clear: When A clears, he and A1 revert to defence, while D and D1 change from defence to attack.

CHANGE FROM ATTACK TO DEFENCE AND VICE-VERSA

ATTACK TO DEFENCE

Whichever player lifts the shuttle, by lob or clear, instead of hitting down, moves back to the centre of the nearest half-court; his less hurried partner moves into the other half-court.

DEFENCE TO ATTACK

The player to whom the shuttle is now hit upwards moves back to attack; his partner *immediately* moves on to T-junction on front service line to maintain attack at net. (If, however, attack is initiated *from half-court* the striker will often follow in his own shot to the net while his partner drops back.) (Fig. 15 &16.)

77

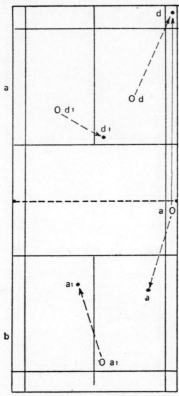

Fig. 16. Transition from attack to defence from lob: When a lobs, he and al revert to defence, while d and d1 change from defence to attack.

GENERAL TACTICS

From the above it will be seen that play can be divided roughly into (a) service and return and (b) attack and defence. Tactics will therefore be described under these headings.

SERVE AND RETURN OF SERVE

LOW SERVE TO CENTRE

The server should probe backhand, body and forehand for a weakness. This serve :

1. Gives receiver least time in which to see it (but conversely, shortest distance to move to it).

78

2. Narrows angle of return, i.e. any return must, theoretically, pass within server's or server's partner's reach (Fig. 17).

RETURN

If taken below tape-height, play:

1. Into body of opposing net player.
2. To corners of net, to open up court, by moving opponent to side line.
3. Low lob, usually deep to backhand.

If taken tape-height or just above, play:

1. Just through advancing server with a brush shot.
2. Half court pushes to side lines (a) to force a lifted reply; (b) to open up the court; (c) to sow doubt between server and partner as to who should return it; or (d) to bring server's partner up and to force server back.
3. Push into right side of server's partner's body to gain a winner or force a cramped reply.
4. Fast pushes into back corners.

If taken well above tape-height, play: down into any gap (Fig. 17).

LOW SERVE TO SIDE LINE

This is:

1. A variant to above.
2. Moves receiver from his base.
3. Moves shuttle away from racquet.
4. Is slightly more difficult to hit, *but*: (a) it is more difficult to serve deceptively and accurately; (b) it opens up the angles dangerously (i.e. shuttle can be hit out of reach or be sharply cross-courted).

This serve is more safely played from the left court because it is on to an opponent's weaker backhand and likely to be returned straight on to the stronger forehand.

RETURNS

Much as above but taking full advantage of the opened angle with deceptive, angled shots across the body, 'held' to the last fraction of a second as alternatives to the likely straight return to which the opponent may already be moving.

FLICK SERVE

This is used as variant to above to (a) drive back receiver from

79

his position dominating the net; (b) to force a weak or defensive return; or (c) occasionally to win a point outright.

1. To the centre: narrows angle of return and gives receiver less time to recover from initial surprise *but* margin of error if aiming too exactly for corner is greater.

2. To the side line: forces receiver wide from base and to some players presents a more difficult return, wide on the forehand, but opens angles and gives receiver more time to recover.

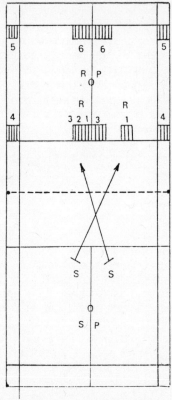

Fig. 17. Placements of doubles serves: 1, 2, 3, 4. Low serves; 5. Flick or high serves; 6. Flick, high or drive serves.

RETURN OF FLICK TO CENTRE

If played early, smash wristily down centre or into body; if a little late, drop into centre or play flat fast clear to backhand; if very late, high deep clear to give time to recover to a defensive

80

position. If server follows service into net, smash steeply at him, eschew all drops, or clear deep, away from his partner.

HIGH SERVE

This is used as a variant to low and flick serves if the latter are not working or servers are strong in defence and opponents are weak in attack. It should be used to garner a few quick points and then be put back in cold storage for emergency use. It is useful in breaking up tempo of game.

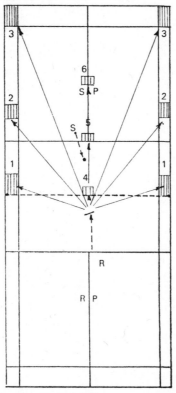

Fig. 18. Returns of service in doubles: 1. and 4. Net shots; 2. Half-court pushes; 3. Fast, deep pushes; 5. Brush shot (on back); 6. Straight push into chest.

It may be hit HIGH (18-20ft) or VERY HIGH (up to 30ft). The advantage of the latter serve is that

1. It is more difficult to time.

2. It is more difficult to hit cleanly since it now drops vertically and not in a parabola.

81

Arguments for placement to side or centre are as for the flick.

Smash steeply into gap or into body. Vary with very occasional well concealed slow drops or fast clears. Particularly in returning very high serve do not overhit or points will be given away.

DRIVE SERVE
Hit fast and low at opponent's face or up his backhand – this is another 'mixer'. It may be played from normal base or from side line. When served from the latter, the server is badly out of position but gains a much greater angle of attack on a weak backhand. (This shot may similarly be played backhanded to a lefthander in the left court.) It may be mixed with (for surprise):
  1. A fast, low serve, cross-court, to the junction of side line and front service line or
  2. A high, cross-court serve to junction of side line and back service line, especially if receiver has taken up stance for backhand return.

RETURNS
To drive from centre court: round-the-head smash into server's body, or drop shots.
  To drive from side line: move back slightly and try round-the-head smash; if errors result and receiver is left off balance, take up backhand stance and play flat clear to backhand corner or drop shot to centre. Much depends on the positioning of server's partner.

After all low serves (and effective flicks and drives), server must move quickly into net base to attack all net-shots, half-court pushes and drives. Server's partner must be equally alert to sustain the attack, or if the serve was a poor one, to keep the shuttle in play.

ATTACK

FROM BETWEEN BASE LINE AND BACK DOUBLES SERVICE LINE
  1. Slow drop-shot: played to centre to cause confusion or nearer slower or less effective player.
  2. Fast clear: played just low enough to avoid interception to backhand or to slower or weaker player, if drop shot is being anticipated.

3. Half-smash or cut smash: used sparingly, and angled and placed so as to maintain attack.

All three shots seek to elicit short return rather than score outright winner (Fig. 19).

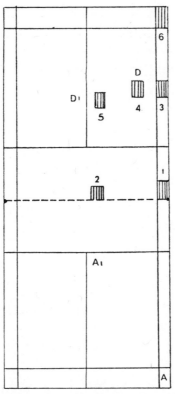

Fig. 19. Placements for attack from side of court: *Drop shots*: 1 and 2. *Smashes*: 3. Side line; 4. D's body; 5. Into gap; *Fast clear*: 6. To backhand.

FROM BETWEEN BACK DOUBLES SERVICE LINE AND
FRONT SERVICE LINE

1. Smash (a) into right side of body of nearer player; (b) into a gap.

Beware of cross-courting and always consider the angle of the likely return: shots into the body, played under pressure, tend to be returned cross-court following the natural fore- or backhand swing. Vary speed of sequence of smashes.

83

2. Drives: as above but beware of driving at a well placed defence: the return is very quick and the attack may be lost.

3. Drops and fast clears may be used as occasional deceptive variants.

FROM FRONT SERVICE LINE TO NET

Racquet must be kept at tape-height.

1. The shuttle is dabbed into gaps or into the body; steep angle is far more important than speed since a fast *flat* dab will fly to the opponent's racquet or out of court.

2. Dead racquet shot played by letting the shuttle hit the racquet, held in a relaxed grip, so that the shuttle drops almost vertically off the racquet, very near the net.

NB. In cross-court smashes or drops, remember the shuttle has farther to travel so giving opponent more time and reducing sting of shot, and it also opens up angles of return. Cross-court sparingly unless there is an obvious gap. Never cross-court net shots or drives unless (a) opponents have been first lured to side line to prevent easy interception; (b) it is possible to hit down or, at worst, flat.

DEFENCE

FROM BETWEEN BASE LINE AND DOUBLES BACK SERVICE LINE

Clear: if off-balance, clear straight, deep and very high to give time for recovery to defensive base.

FROM BETWEEN DOUBLES BACK SERVICE LINE AND FRONT SERVICE LINE

1. Return of smash or drive by (a) lob – high enough to avoid interception and so placed as to run smasher from side to side hurriedly (off steep smash); (b) drop shot to corners of net; (c) push past net player to half-court; (d) drive – fast cross-court or into smasher's body (off flat smash); or (e) dab (off flat smash) – move well up to net, and crouching, dab shuttle steeply down into body or gap.

2. Return of push shot: (a) if still at tape height, use another push; (b) if lower, a very accurate net shot, generally straight.

FROM BETWEEN FRONT SERVICE LINE AND NET

1. Lob – if shuttle is taken only a foot or so from the floor,

hit very high if time is needed to regain balance; if not, hit only high enough to avoid interception and from side to side of court to hurry opponent into error.

2. Net shot – if shuttle is taken within a foot of the tape, play up accurately to one of corners. Don't panic and lob.

LADIES' DOUBLES

These are played according to the principles above but

1. As their smashes are less strong than men's they smash less, using instead more good length clears and drops to make a clear cut opening or force an error.

2. High serves may be used with less danger but so too may the low serve as few ladies toe the line to receive.

MAXIMS

Shots down the middle: if low, take on the backhand; if high, on the forehand. All defensive strokes seek to regain attack. All 'rules' are variable according to circumstance and players' abilities; no rule is inflexible.

MIXED DOUBLES

COURT POSITIONS

OPENING POSITIONS

These differ from those outlined for men's and ladies' doubles as follows:

1. When the man serves, he stands 5–7ft behind the front service line so that he is then virtually on his main base. His partner always stands on or just in front of the front service line and as near the centre line as she can, in the *left* court. (This keeps the girl centrally situated and, with frying pan grip, she can take almost all shots forehanded.)

2. When the man receives, the lady will generally stand in her court on or just in front of the front service line and as near the centre line as possible. Some men prefer the lady to stand slightly to the rear of them. From here, she can quickly move in to the net when the man withdraws from it or move to cover the back of the court if the man stays at the net to maintain and clinch his attack.

3. When the lady serves or receives, the basic positions previously described in men's and ladies' doubles are adopted.

SUBSEQUENT POSITIONS
A back and front position is generally adopted. It is therefore of paramount importance to seize and maintain the attack. A sides formation is used only where the lady is exceptionally strong, the equal of a man.

The slower and less powerful lady covers the whole width of one-third of the court between the net and the front service line; the stronger and faster man covers the whole width of two-thirds of the court between front service line and base line. A gap of more than 6ft between them can become a target area.

SERVE AND RETURN

SERVING
This is basically the same as in men's and ladies' doubles. There are, however, these differences:

1. The high serve is seldom used to the man as the opposing man has to cover the likely smash, placed to either side line. It is used against the opposing lady to drive her from her net base if she is not strong overhead.

2. The fast flat drive, particularly down the centre line on to the lady's backhand, or into a gap, is used more frequently.

RETURN OF SERVE
The lady, if a little slow, replies with upward net shot; if fast, she tries the half-court push. The man should always seek to hit down to gain the initial ascendancy. Since, however, he must (unless he has a very strong partner) get back to cover the back of the court he does so with a little restraint and always so places his shot that the likely return leaves him or his partner the shortest distance to move to it.

Both in return of serve, and in serve, the man and the lady concentrate on harassing the lady as much as possible – she is the weak link which may crack.

BASIC TACTICS

Because the man has the difficult task of covering the whole width of the back court, the basic consideration in mixed doubles is not to lift the shuttle, so putting the opponents on the attack. Thus after service and its return as above, both sides employ net

86

shots and half-court pushes in a tentative probing to force one
of them to lift the shuttle to a greater or lesser degree. Be it less,
the man uses the fast drive; be it more, the hunt is on, and
smashes and fast drops are the order of the day. The attack
must be maintained (Plates 49 and 50).

THE MAN

ATTACK

1. Returning a slightly lofted or too deep push the man will
drive: (a) hard and straight into the man's body or the back
'box'; (b) if opponents have been lured to side line he will drive
fast cross-court – more safely from left to right than right to
left (Fig. 20).

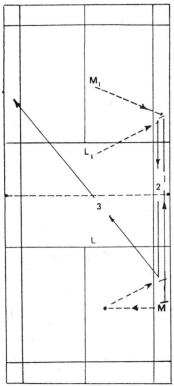

Fig. 20. Cross-courting: M's well-placed and disguised half-court push (1)
elicits slightly high return (2) and draws M1 and L1 to side of court. Only then
does M cross-court (3).

2. If the shuttle is lofted to back doubles service line he will smash steeply to the side lines, straight or occasionally cross-court, or to the man's body.

3. If the shuttle is lofted deep to the base line, he will generally play fast drops to the side lines so harassing the opposing lady or drawing up her partner. These shots may occasionally be varied with steep, angled, smashes played well within himself.

DEFENCE

1. If he has to take half-court shots below tape height he will reply with net shots or return half-court pushes; occasionally with a concealed low lob deep to the backhand.

2. In returning drives, he will, if well placed and balanced, play drives; if he needs to slow the pace, pushes, to tempt the lady to 'nibble', or net shots.

3. In returning smashes, he will drive into gaps or the smasher's body if possible but more likely will have to be content with accurate net shots or pushes.

THE LADY

At all times, she must keep her racquet up at tape height, seek to take the shuttle at the earliest possible moment, and narrow the angle. "Stop" shots from a "dead" racquet are invaluable.

ATTACK

She should take only those shots which she can comfortably control, i.e. those in front of the ears! Those she cannot take can be played by her partner moving in, with more time in which to see the shuttle and to make his stroke. Any shots an inch or more above the tape she will dab *down* crisply and steeply into gaps between the two opponents or into the body, with a minimum of backswing. She *must* avoid flat returns that go out or straight to the man's racquet (Plate 50).

DEFENCE

Shots taken below tape height should be met with answering net shots, just over the tape; only occasionally or if in real trouble should deep but low lobs to the backhand be used.

Drives should either be dabbed downwards or angled away with a push shot or dealt with by a dead racquet shot. If met early, fast drops may be dabbed down or angled away; if late, push or net shots will be used.

The following are important points best dealt with separately.

PARTICULAR TACTICS

HIGH SERVE TO LADY
If the girl is quickly back, she should half-smash or fast drop steeply to a gap, so placing the shot as to try and force any net reply back to her side of the court. She immediately moves in to cover three-quarters of the net; the distant quarter must, if necessary, be covered by her partner. If she is slow, she will probably have little option but to clear very high and very deep or play a fast clear to the backhand.

ANGLED SERVE TO LADY'S BACKHAND
The man, when serving from the right will sometimes serve fast and flat from the outside side line to the junction of centre line and back doubles service line. If possible she takes this round her head and hits it into the body or a gap. If she cannot play round-the-head shots, she should take up a backhand stance (though not forgetting the outside corners), and drive or lift the shuttle to the far side line.

LADY BEHIND MAN WHEN HE RECEIVES
If an aggressive receiver of serve, with a strong partner, does not score an outright winner, he may stay in at the net to intercept the return(s). Should the shuttle pass him, the lady will play out the rally as a man, or, play a steep half-smash or fast drop. Calling 'Back!' to her partner, she follows it in whilst he regains his normal mid-court base (Fig. 21).

DEFENCE
Some pairs, even when threatened with a smash, stay strictly back and front. Others adopt a different system: the lady moves right into the net cross-court from the striker, some 3-4ft from the centre line. From here, she tries to pick off the (slightly slower) cross-court smash, as well as dealing with drop shots. The man moves over to take the (faster) straight smash and straight drops, if need be.

Attack against such defence can be fivefold: (a) steep smash slightly to left of or straight at girl; (b) straight smash at man's body; (c) straight drop; (d) smash between man and girl; (e) fast low clear over girl (Fig. 22 and Plate 51).

89

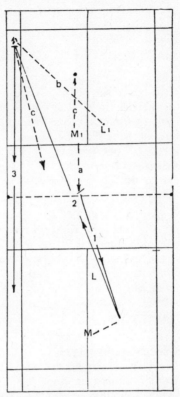

Fig. 21. Lady drops back to cover man when he rushes serve: When M1 is drawn right into net (a) and plays ineffective push (1), L1 drops back (b), plays a half smash (3), and comes into net (c) as M1 regains base (c).

SINGLES

OPENING COURT POSITIONS

Server generally stands about 4-5ft behind front service line, and a foot or so from centre line.

Receiver generally stands about 5-6ft behind front service line : 2-3ft from centre-line in the left court, near it in the right court.

BASIC COURT POSITION

Each player has a base on the centre line, about 4-6ft behind the front service line, dependent on his speed of movement and strength of backhand.

This is varied in the following way to cut down the opponent's

90

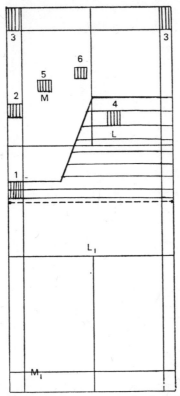

Fig. 22. Attack against wedge defence: M1 can play: *Drop shot*, 1. *Smashes*: side line, 2. Into body, 4 and 5. Into gap, 6. *Fast clears*, 3.

angle of return. If the player hits a shuttle to his opponent's forehand side line, he will move his base 12-18 inches to that side; similarly, if the shuttle is hit to the backhand side, he moves 12-18 inches to that side. If the player's drops or net shots are very tight, his base may be advanced a foot or so. He should generally move quickly back to the appropriate base after each stroke (Fig. 23).

SERVICE

The majority of serves are hit high to the base line within a couple of feet of its junction with the centre line to narrow the angle of return. When the player serves to the left court, he may serve wider to the side line to make attack on his own backhand more difficult. The low serve, even when well concealed,

91

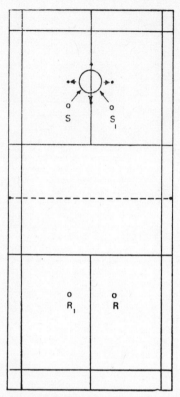

Fig. 23. Basic positions in singles: Receiver's and server's positions; also variable main base to which server moves.

is employed only rarely and then by players with a backhand strong enough to resist the ensuing attack on it. High serves should be varied in height and placement. Drives may be used occasionally if opponent (or his racquet) is badly positioned or he reacts slowly (Fig. 24).

RETURN OF SERVE

A good-length high serve will be returned either with a deep clear, a cut smash, or a slow drop, generally to the corners. A low serve will be played, deceptively, tight to the net or lobbed low and fast to the backhand. It should seldom be rushed unless an outright winner is certain (Fig. 25).

GENERAL PLAY

Clears, like serves, will be countered with clears (a war of

92

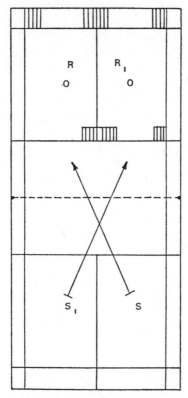

Fig. 24. Placements of singles serves.

accurate and consistent attrition) varied with slow drop shots. By such shots, varied and played to the corners, the opponent is forced to run the maximum distance from corner to corner until an opening is made or an error forced.

Generally players are weaker in the deep backhand corner so every effort is made to attack this; sometimes it is best exposed by first playing shots to the forehand.

When the shuttle is cleared or lobbed to, or short of, the back doubles service line, a steep smash to the side line, or into the right side of the body, is played. This may be varied, from a little deeper in court by cut smashes which deceptively fade away to the side line. Smash should be cross-court only when opponent is out of position. A smash should never be played that will leave the striker off balance.

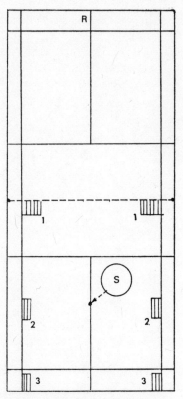

Fig. 25. Placements of returns of high serves (or clears): 1. Floating drop shots; 2. Half-smashes; 3. Clears.

Drop shots are returned by two different strokes. If the shuttle is played near the floor, a deep high lob is generally the best answer. If the shuttle can be taken (a) above tape-height, the dab is used; (b) up to 6 inches below tape-height, the stab; (c) more than 6 inches below, the upward net shot, ideally, just crawling over the tape, or, if the opponent is not quick into the net, the hair-pin. These net shots in return are countered by similar net shots or fast low lobs to the base line.

Singles is thus basically a succession of well disguised deep clears and lobs and tight drop shots with net shots interspersed. Clears and lobs will be high or low according to whether the striker needs time or is forcing the pace. Long sparring like this may be necessary before a winner is made. Such a sequence of

94

shots should be varied so that no regular pattern is established. (Fig. 26).

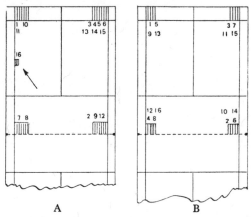

Fig. 26. Sequence of shots in singles: A. Well varied: B. Too stereotyped.

Essential qualities for the singles player are patience, persistence, and, therefore, fitness; speed of foot; strong backhand clear; consistent length with serves, clears and drops; net shots that just crawl over the tape; and quick perception of opponent's weaknesses in footwork, tactics and strokes.

BASIC GENERAL TACTICS FOR ALL GAMES

1. Lift the shuttle as little as possible (except in singles).
2. Maintain the attack at all costs (a) by moving to the shuttle, (b) by hitting *down* whenever possible.
3. Play either right into the body or into gaps first created by running opponents about over full width and length of court.
4. Cross-court sparingly, when opponent has been manoeuvred out of position, and even then don't hit upwards.
5. Always seek to regain base between shots.
6. Play on the weaker or slower player.
7. Open up and attack the backhand.
8. CONCENTRATE and so avoid unforced errors.

COMMON TACTICAL ERRORS AND THEIR CORRECTION

All the tactical maxims set out above and in Chapter 9 will frequently be honoured more in the breach than in the observance.

95

They are best observed by the coach if he:

1. Ignores all incidental stroke production errors.

2. Does not become mesmerized by the game itself, the score, the flight of the shuttle and the whole swiftly moving ballet.

3. Watches first one player, then his partner, and finally how the two dovetail as a pair.

4. Watches (a) service and its return; (b) return of service and its return; (c) attack both at the net and at the back; (d) defence. Even for this, he may need to watch each player in turn.

The errors observed may best be corrected in any, or a combination, of the five following ways, according to need and the time available.

1. The error is logically explained and/or the coach demonstrates how other tactics are much more effective.

2. The rally is replayed correctly several times.

3. The opponent's last stroke and the player's corrected error are rehearsed as a brief routine.

4. A conditioned game is evolved which repeats the situation often.

5. A game is played in which the player concentrates solely on correcting this one error.

Mere verbal correction is never sufficient.

NET SHOTS

2 Down: Margaret Allen, with controlled care, dabs shuttle steeply and crisply down with light uncocking of wrist

3 Upwards (forehand): the Author delicately strokes the shuttle to make it crawl just over the net; taken tape high; eyes on shuttle; leaning in to shot: great concentration

34 Upwards (backhand): the Author takes the shuttle ideally tape-high; well balanced, he leans slightly into stroke

35   36

HIGH SERVE

35 Position of readiness: weight on back foot; racquet well back, arm bent and wrist cocked; shuttle between thumb and forefinger, at shoulder height, in front of left foot; eyes gauging distance

36 Arm straightening, but wrist still cocked; weight on front foot – but oh those eyes!

37

38

37 Impact: arm nearly straight: wrist uncocking: eyes now down (thank goodness!)

38 Follow-through: long and strong over right shoulder

RETURN OF SERVE
39 Stance: Ray Sharp, toeing the front line, crouched, knees bent as springs, weight on the balls of the well spaced feet, racquet at tape-height, eyes observantly on server, is perfectly poised for instant movement forwards or backwards

       41

40 Hitting down: launching himself forward Ray meets the shuttle at the tape to play it down with a brush shot

41 Hitting up: taken unusually late for Ray, he exemplifies absolute controlled care and concentration as he plays a tape-hugging backhand return into the incoming server's body

42

43

44

THE LOB (BACKHAND)

42 Sue Whetnall, a picture of eager alertness keeps her eye on falling shuttle as she moves in with right foot forward, elbow bent, wrist cocked, racquet head at shoulder level

43 Just before impact: final long stride leaves right leg well bent and left outstretched; arm is nearly straight but wrist still cocked back

44 Follow-through: leaning into the shot and keeping her head down fractionally, Sue sweeps the racquet head at target area and then up above head height

45

45 Tyna Barinaga has been forced to take the shuttle even later at absolute full stretch and rather wide

MEN'S DOUBLES

46 Basic opening positions: Ian Cornfoot (Canterbury Pilgrims) serves from near centre line; Ray Sharp perfectly poised to receive; the Author crouches with racquet in front of vulnerable body to intercept fast or half-court pushes; Paul Whetnall in equally alert position of readiness

47 Attack and defence: Paul Whetnall at back smashes straight; partner Ray Sharp, racquet raised, confident of his ability to move in fast, stands behind T-junction; defenders, tensely poised to take shuttle backhanded, have moved across to left to narrow angle of return

9

ANALYSIS OF STROKES
AND TACTICS

STROKE ANALYSIS

Many coaches and players find it hard to analyse a doubles game. It is indeed difficult to do so for all of the players or even for one pair if they are beyond the stage of making obvious mistakes. The following chart has therefore been devised to help concentration on one player at a time. A game should be chosen in which the student is playing against a slightly better player.

There are three different methods which can be employed:

1. A stroke is put in the appropriate column whenever a rally is won or lost by the student.

2. A much truer picture will emerge if the following additional procedure is adopted:

(a) The student's winners and losers are ignored if they stem mainly from his partner's last stroke, e.g. if the student makes an easy kill from the weak return of a very good smash by his partner, or he fails to return a smash after a very poor clear by his partner.

(b) The student's own previous shot is marked down if this, rather than the actual winning or losing shot, is the cause of the end of the rally, e.g. a mark is put under 'Drop' not 'Smash' if he makes a simple kill from a weak return of his own very accurate drop; or a mark is put under 'Serve' rather than 'Return of Smash' if he cannot get back a smash from his own very bad length high serve.

3. A further refinement is to mark down the following symbols rather than just a stroke:

D = If deception ended the rally.
N = If the shuttle was hit into the net
O = If the shuttle was hit out of court.
S = If speed or slowness caused the end of the rally.

This may sound complicated but with a little practice it enables the coach to give a true assessment and sound advice rather than mutter vague generalities. Where an obvious weakness appears it must be analysed to see if its cause is technique or tactics.

STROKE ANALYSIS CHART

PLAYERS : N. Brown and Miss P. Green v S. White and Miss P. Grey.

SCORE : 8-15, 10-15.

PLAYER : N. Brown.

Stroke	Won		Lost		Comments
	Forehand	Backhand	Forehand	Backhand	
Clear	1		11	1O11lO1	Slow moving and late backswing; could take as forehand drop.
Drive	11S	1	11111111	111N11N	Cross-courts too soon and often.
Drop	1D1111D	1	1O	NOON11	Drop well disguised; late backswing on backhand.
Lob					

Net shot
  Hit down
  Hit up
	11
	1				

Serve
  Drive
  Flick
  Low
	111111111
	D1
	1
			OO
			111111
			11111
					Attacks lady's backhand; flick given away by longer backswing.

Return of serve
  Hit down
  Hit up
	S1S111S
	1
		1	NN
			1
				11	Uses reach well.

98

Smash	11S1111		NNONN11		Powerful, but played too often when off balance.
Return of smash	111111	1	1	NN	Good eye and reach help him push and drive effectively.

D = Deception; N = Hit into net; O = Hit out of court; S = Speed or Slowness

CORRECTIONS

SLUGGISH MOVEMENT

1. Agility exercises to music.

2. Practice of drops fed slightly to backhand but taken on forehand.

3. Conditioned game: no backhand clears only drops.

LATE BACKSWING

Individual practice: call 'Back!' to help earlier backswing while moving into position.

CROSS-COURTING

Conditioned Games:

1. No cross-courting.

2. No cross-courting until at least two straight shots have been played.

OBVIOUS FLICK

Practice of alternate low and flick serves. (Place chair at point where Brown's backswing for low serve finishes to prevent longer swing for flick.)

TACTICAL ANALYSIS

Each coach should similarly make out his own tactical analysis chart incorporating the following points. These, together with the stroke analysis chart will complete the whole picture of a player's ability.

SINGLES

(a) Consistency of length; (b) variation of height and placement of serve and return of serve; (c) exploiting and narrowing angle of return; (d) cross-courting; (e) use of height in clears and lobs to gain and to seize time; (f) variation of tempo and 'pattern of shots'; (g) opening up and attacking backhand; (h) attack directed into gaps or the body but smash used sparingly in singles only; (i) economic use of round-the-head shots; (j) deception by similarity of basic strokes; (k) recovery on balance to base before each return is played; (l) finding and playing on weakness, and realizing one's own errors; (m) tight net shots.

MEN'S AND LADIES' DOUBLES
(a), (c), (d), (e), (f), (g), (h), (j), (k) and (l) apply here also. In addition: (m) use of occasional high serves or clears to break up tempo; (n) playing shots to elicit return to a desired side; (o) both players maintaining the attack both from initial serve and return and later from smashes and drops; (p) seizing attack from a defensive position.

MIXED DOUBLES
(c), (d), (f), (g), (h), (i), (j), (k), (l), (n), (o) and (p) all apply. In addition: (q) attack on lady's serve; (r) attack on lady by pin-pointed serving; (s) controlled and thoughtful rushing of serve by man with possible return to him or his partner borne in mind; (t) using steepness and angle rather than sheer power of shot; (u) keeping shuttle low; (v) sound defensive agreement; (w) effective use of half-court shots; (x) moving in to take shuttle early; (y) using full width of court; (z) playing for partner.

100

10

ONLY *PERFECT* PRACTICE
MAKES PERFECT

Since actual practice is 80-90% of a lesson it must be effective. The coach should give it as much care and thought as he does his exposition and questioning. All practices must be specific, realistic, economical and enjoyable. 'Practice makes permanent – but only perfect practice makes perfect' is a maxim that both students and coach should always bear in mind.

ORDER OF TEACHING STROKES

This must be logical, progressing from basic to specialist, and from simple to difficult strokes. Where possible, one stroke should be the foundation for the next: e.g. clear to smash; low serve to flick. To double work done they should be learnt and practised complementarily: e.g. drop and lob; smash and push return. No order can satisfy all criteria but the one on page 29 does cover most of these points.

ORGANIZATION

This, if crisp and unobtrusive, should lead to a self-disciplined class. Safety is a paramount consideration; it is achieved through : (a) not overcrowding a court; (b) accurate feeding; (c) staggering strikers; (d) placing left-handers on left for forehand shots and on right for backhand shots; (e) strict insistence that mishits are not chased. Players should be positioned on court by lucid instructions, by name, and, if necessary, by hand! Shuttles must be shared fairly and returned to base after each practice. Such return, by coach and players alike, should be brisk (Plates 52 and 53).

Whether classes should be divided into 'Good' and 'Bad'

101

sections or whether egalitarianism should prevail is always a vexed question. To avoid stultification of both categories, each will generally practise with players of comparable ability, but better players must be prepared in the early stages to help with the feeding of their weaker brethren. On the other hand the class may be kept as one group playing the same shot but at different levels of attainment or it may be split to allow better players to move on to a new stroke.

MOTIVATION

In the final analysis, success depends on the student's whole-hearted determination and co-operation. He must, therefore, be constantly motivated. The coach must turn psychologist and know the best baits to dangle. He must find out if the student wishes to play in order to (a) win admiration of his fellows or parents, a girl or even the coach himself; (b) keep fit; (c) achieve power over himself – and others; (d) play for his country, so touring abroad and hitting the headlines; (e) be one of a socially acceptable group; (f) meet the opposite sex; (g) perfect a skill; (h) have fun. The perceptive coach should find out what makes each student tick.

COMPETITION

This is so basic a form of motivation that it must be dealt with separately. The better players will be stimulated by competing, each with a chance of success, against one another. Poorer players may be discouraged by this and should therefore compete mainly against their own previous best results.

KNOWLEDGE OF RESULTS

Practice without a clear realization of the aim or with no appreciation of success or failure can lead only to boredom. The more immediate and exact this appreciation is, the better the student will learn. A ready appreciation of the sensuous ease of a well timed stroke, and of the crisp 'crack' accompanying it, the coach's swift 'Good shot!' and clear targets are essential if the student is to improve.

SUCCESS

Knowledge of success is the greatest motivator of all. Success, remember, is relevant to the learner's ambitions. The coach must show his student a number of shallow steps leading to a

102

clearly discernible, attainable, and worthwhile goal. Their ascent will be achieved through good facilities, not too ambitious coaching, handicapping, routines that are not too demanding, and few but large targets. Over-long plateaux (periods of no improvement) are the result of poor coaching, lack of fitness or incentive, staleness, or a change to new techniques.

FEEDING

Accurate feeding is essential. It may be done, (a) by the coach alone or (b) by the student(s) who:
  (i) merely drop the shuttle to the racquet;
  (ii) throw the shuttle, using where possible an action similar to the action of the stroke being played (Plate 57).
  (iii) hit the shuttle, using a correct stroke to do so.
  The coach must demonstrate clearly the height and placement of the shuttle for feeding each stroke. He must check that feeding is done well and that its importance is fully appreciated. The need for care at all times and a racquet head aimed at the target should be stressed. At first, feeding should be slow and deliberate to give the striker ample time to prepare for the next shot. As the striker progresses, feeding may be speeded up. Placing of the shuttle should also be progressive. That is to say, the shuttle is first fed exactly on to the striker's racquet. Later the shuttle is fed farther and farther from the racquet so that the striker learns to play while on the move.

TARGETS

These will vary in size according to the students' skill; they should always be large enough to ensure some successful, but not too easy, results. A multiplicity of them is readily available. Formal archery-type targets can be used on walls, or, more simply, sheets of coloured paper or chalked targets. The most effective floor targets are the lines themselves, or areas bounded by them or by additional chalked lines. Other readily available targets, easily adapted for size, are newspapers, towels or tracksuits; boxes or tins make a more satisfying 'plonk'. Other players used as targets for smashes make use of our inherent sadism as motivation! Hoops, suspended above the court or laid on the floor, are challenging. Fixed to the net, they may be used also as an alternative to a cord stretched above the net, for checking the height of low serves, drives or net shots.

PRACTICE ON COURT

WHOLE OR PART METHOD

Opinion is divided as to whether a stroke should be learnt as a whole or by parts.

Whole Method. When a stroke is not too complex, the whole method is undoubtedly the better; it is more economical of time, more natural and fluent, and avoids plateaux. With harder strokes it can lead to failure and consequent loss of motivation.

Part Method. For a beginner, a smash is a most complex neuro-muscular action. A small racquet head must be swept along a complicated course to meet a still smaller shuttle flying on an unusual trajectory at a tiny point of impact with split-second exactitude of timing! He may therefore learn more easily if the stroke is broken into its component parts: (a) backswing; (b) forward swing and impact; (c) follow-through and recovery. If impact and recovery were treated as separate parts, the action would be over-simplified. These three parts can be taught in different ways (Plate 52).

1. (a), (b) and (c) are each learnt separately and then joined.
2. (a) is learnt and then (b); (b) is joined to (a); (c) is learnt then joined to (a) and (b) combined.
3. (a) is learnt; (b) is learnt with (a); (c) is learnt with (a) and (b).
4. (b) is learnt first; (c) is added to it; and finally (a) is added to (b) and (c).

Such simplification can give the less able some early success but takes longer all told; weaknesses tend to occur at the joins, progress is slowed by plateaux and the stroke may be stiff and stilted.

SPEED AND ACCURACY

It is generally desirable to teach free-flowing strokes (overheads and drives, etc.) at as fast a speed as is compatible with success, especially where speed is the essence of that stroke. Slowing them down too much creates different and incorrect strokes; accuracy so gained is often lost when the stroke is speeded up. Playing all out leads to repeated errors, defeat and disillusion. A happy medium should therefore be sought by the novice. The desired consistency and accuracy can be achieved comparatively simply by reasonable care and aiming the racquet head at the target area.

LENGTH AND FREQUENCY

Too long a practice leads to mental and physical fatigue; for a beginner, learning a new stroke can be exhausting. Weariness brings errors which are hard to eradicate later. Too short a practice is equally frustrating and leads to little improvement. Optimum learning in the initial stages is achieved by frequent short practices. It will be found that 10 minutes is probably the maximum length of useful consecutive practice of one stroke for the average adult. Where the practice is going well, it may be carried on a little longer than this but should be stopped even earlier if obvious physical or mental fatigue set in.

PROGRESSION

Though practices should start without being too demanding they must gradually become ever harder. Initially, a beginner, with racquet head in the small of his back, will have the shuttle hit straight to him and gain a 'point' if he merely clears it over the net. Years later, by a dozen progressions, he will have become able to play twenty consecutive clears right to the base line, and be running in to the front service line and back between shots.

Such progressions are achieved by continually demanding: (a) greater fluency of stroke; (b) greater accuracy on decreasing target areas (outspread *Times* to folded *Daily Mirror*); (c) better length; (d) less and less net clearance; (e) greater number of repetitions; (f) more movement between shots; (g) more and more pressure from threatening opponents (e.g. in the low serve, practice starts with no opponent; then receiver is placed well back merely to threaten, gradually moving nearer the net, until eventually he actually attacks the serve).

When such progressions are rapid it must be readily appreciated by the student in order to add more fuel to the fires of his ambition. When progress is minimal, some students respond by going back to a simpler skill, others by racing ahead to a harder one, and still others by merely 'thinking' a shot correctly.

PRACTICE OFF COURT

The brain receives signals in the form of electrical impulses along nerves from its receptors: eyes, ears, nose (the latter little used in badminton!). In reaction to these stimuli similar impulses are sent from the brain via the spinal cord to the muscle fibres, for each of these thousands of striated fibres has its own nerve.

The speed at which these impulses travel cannot be increased, but the intervals between them can be shortened. This is achieved when the nerves learn the pattern required; the speed-up is thought to occur at the junction of incoming and outcoming nerves, known as the synapse.

This learning by the nerves is achieved when a stroke is grooved. This can be done by actual practice on court or by thought off court. It has been proved that if a player can 'think' a shot or sequence of shots correctly, the same nerve impulses occur as when he actually plays them. It is the nervous system's exact control of muscle movement that we call timing or co-ordination or quick reflex.

HANDICAPPING AND INCENTIVES

To encourage more positive effort handicapping may be used. This can be done in a variety of ways to give the 'bunny' that heady and essential whiff of success. Points and 'hands' (serves) can be given or owed. Better players can be restricted in the shots they can use (e.g. no smash or no flick service). Similarly, their movement can be restricted to walking (excellent for anticipation) or they may have to end a rally in a specified number of shots or play to a nominated part of their opponents' court. Individual bonus points may be given by the coach for a point won by a particular stroke or skill (e.g. half-court push return of serve, smash into body, flick serve, speed or deception, correct cross-courting). Similarly, points can be lost for a careless, unforced error or such bad tactics as unnecessarily lifting the shuttle or cross-courting rashly.

11

PRACTICES

Practices such as the following examples are an integral part of coaching either a small group or a large class. Used for only part of a coaching session, they will by their very novelty and variety, as opposed to more routine stroke practices, help maintain interest. In group coaching of beginners, they are an essential means of occupying large numbers in a one-court hall. They may be used purely for practice or competitively but they must be enjoyable and realistic. They should be chosen according to the players' needs and abilities, to the space available, and to numbers. The coach will be able to devise many more examples to suit his own particular circumstances.

CO-ORDINATION PRACTICES

Children and adult novices often find co-ordination difficult at first. The following exercises with balls not only helps overcome this problem but also lends variety.

WITHOUT A RACQUET

1. In pairs, static at first, later on the move: players throw old shuttles overhand to each other to catch. To assist in achieving correct throwing action, a shuttle is placed behind the thrower's right heel so that he has to sweep down and back before bending arm and cocking wrist to complete backswing.

2. Pairs, moving, bounce a ball between them; the ball is thrown a little way away from the partner who must catch it first bounce before quickly returning it in the same way.

3. In pairs: A stands 6ft from, and facing, a 10ft section of wall. B, 6ft behind A, throws ball at various heights, angles and speeds against wall. A tries to intercept rebound; if he fails, B must recover ball on first bounce.

4. In pairs: A stands 10-15ft from B who has his back to him. As A throws ball to B, A calls 'Bill!'. B turns swiftly to catch ball. (Delay calling longer and vary trajectory ball.)

5. In threes or groups: one player tries to intercept ball bounced between the others.

6. A game of badminton is played using an air-flow ball only. It is thrown and must be caught before it hits the floor. It must be returned over the net from exactly the same height and place as that at which it was caught (e.g. below tape – upwards, underarm; tape-height – flat, side-arm; above tape-height – downwards or upwards, overarm). Technique and tactics are thus practised simultaneously at a simple level.

WITH A RACQUET

1. Player, holding racquet, in shortened grip and with bent arm, feeds himself by hitting shuttle up (about 6ft) and trying

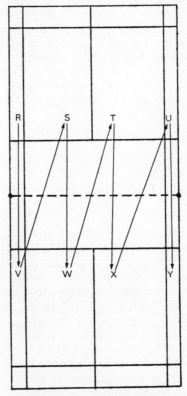

Fig. 27. Simple push shots.

to maintain a sequence of hits. As his confidence increases, he lengthens grip and straightens arm. He also varies height to which shuttle is hit (1-20ft) and walks about as he hits. Further, he alternates between forehand and backhand shots. This practice, which accustoms the beginner to the length of his new 'arm', can be made into a race or team relay. It also enables the player to see the relationship of racquet and shuttle to each other all the time.

2. Six to eight players form a circle or are spaced down the sides of hall. They hit shuttle underhand to any other player in the group (or to coach). Team aim is to get the biggest number of hits without shuttle touching the ground.

3. As above but players start with racquet between shoulder-blades and clear to each other or the coach.

4. Players are spaced along both sides of the net and about 8ft from it. Crouching a little, with racquet vertical, they play push shots up and down the line to one another (Fig. 27).

5. Rounders in teams. Bowler throws shuttle in any way to striker who may hit with any stroke, forehand or backhand. Fielders catch and throw shuttle to base to run out striker. 'Circuit' should be short and different types of running practised.

6. In pairs: A hits shuttle underhand to B who catches or cradles shuttle on racquet face by drawing it under shuttle at the latter's speed. This develops 'feel'.

7. Air-flow ball or shuttle is suspended from ceiling, beam or girder so that student can reach it to play a clear only with a straight arm.

THROWING PRACTICES

1. In pairs: students, facing each other across the width of the court, throw the shuttle as for (a) forehand clear; (b) backhand clear; (c) forehand drive; (d) backhand drive (backhand 'shots' should be played with the thumb inside the shuttle).

2. As above, but each player has a shuttle. Having thrown the shuttles, both players run forward to centre of the court, just beyond their partner, then side-step behind him, and run backwards to base as in a country dancing 'Dosey-Do' (Fig. 28).

3. As in (2) above, but with very large numbers; the number of pairs is doubled by having pairs opposite each other on *both* *sides* of the centre line (Fig. 28) (Plate 58).

4. As in (2) or even (3) above, but one player in each pair has racquet and plays clears (drops and lobs) into opposite

wall before advancing as before. Players should be carefully staggered and plenty of shuttles available.

WALL PRACTICES

In these, players can either (a) hit the shuttle at a wall, or (b) rally against a wall. A line should be clearly marked to represent the net tape, and other appropriate targets be set above it.

HITTING AT WALL

1. In groups of two or three: striker faces wall; feeder (and fag) stand with back(s) to wall. Feeder throws shuttle appropriately to striker who plays (a) clear; (b) smash; (c) drop shot;

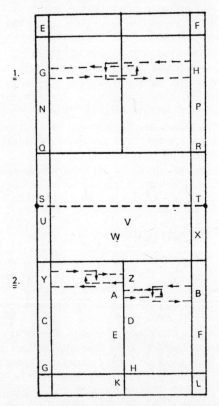

Fig. 28. Throwing practices: (1) H and G throw shuttles simultaneously, catch and advance, or G may play clear. (2) Z and Y, B and A as above but numbers on court are now doubled.

110

(d) drive or (e) lob. Fag catches shuttle on rebound and supplies feeder. NB. Striker should be at as realistic a distance from wall as space and numbers permit. Feeder and fag must be safely positioned (Fig. 2).

2. In pairs, striker and fag: striker practises (a) low (b) flick (c) drive or (d) high serves. For (a) and (c) a line 6-9 inches above tape line should be drawn.

RALLYING AGAINST WALL

One player standing about 6ft from wall:

1. Drive-serves against wall and then plays a succession of lobs from rebounds.

2. High serves against wall and then plays a rally of clears.

3. As above, but smashes, plays lob return, smashes again, etc.

4. Plays a rally of drives.

PRACTICES ON OWN AT HOME

1. Dropping shuttle for service; erect stance and finger grip of shuttle: (a) for low serve, drop shuttle on to small target placed just beside toes of leading foot; (b) for high serve, as above, but place target about a foot farther forward.

2. Shadowing strokes: preferably indoors in front of a mirror, but failing that, in the garden – despite the neighbours' incredulity!

3. Throwing ball under-, over-, or side-arm against a wall and catching it.

4. Grip changing and use of wrist.

5. Wall practices – but only in dead calm.

6. Shadow rallying: playing imaginary rallies on the lawn. (Ursula Smith, the 1965 All-England Champion, did hours of this practice, which is excellent for mobility, stamina, and tactical thought.)

7. Self-feeding by throwing shuttle up from flat racquet face, with feet in correct position for playing whichever shot is to be practised.

8. 'Thinking' a shot after study of a book or photos.
NB. Such a practice should be done when the player is already fairly proficient or, without the coach's guidance, he will merely groove himself incorrectly.

INDIVIDUAL RALLYING PRACTICES

Where the numbers and space permit, ideal basic practice is with two or four players on one court, e.g. A strikes; B feeds;

111

and C and D act as fag or feeder. Positions are changed after ten to twenty shots have been played.

1. B feeds A from mid-court with good high serve: A plays clear; C lets shuttle drop to show length and returns it to B. Similarly with (a) drops shots; (b) smash; (c) overhead backhand shots, and, with appropriate feeding, (d) lobs and (e) drives (Fig. 29).

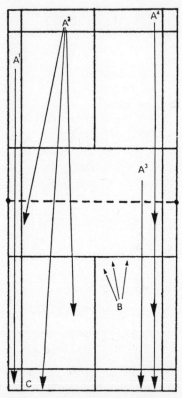

Fig. 29. Rallying practices: A_1 drives; A_2 drops, clears or smashes forehanded; A_3 lobs; A_4 drops, smashes or clears backhanded; B and C place themselves appropriately as feeder and fag.

2. As players make contact consistently and play with some accuracy to reasonable lengths, rallying with complementary shots, first without and then with movement, may be practised: (a) A and B clear to one another; (b) A drops: B lobs; (c) A smashes: B lob returns; (d) A and B exchange drives; (e) A serves: B returns serve; (f) A and B play net shots (Fig. 30).

112

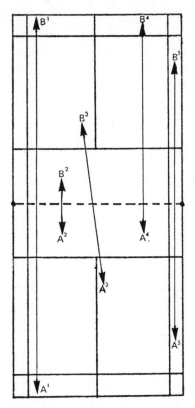

Fig. 30. Complementary shots: $A_1 - B_1$, clears; $A_2 - B_2$, net shots; $A_3 - B_3$, serves and returns; $A_4 - B_4$, lobs and drops; $A_5 - B_5$ drives.

3.. When such general rallying is fairly consistent, really grooved production, footwork, stamina, accuracy and still greater consistency should be practised systematically in this way: A, for realism, moves in and out from a centre base to clear. B, to ensure good feeding, remains on the target area. Each stroke is then practised on both forehand and backhand, and both straight and cross-court. Similar practices can be worked out for (a) smash; (b) drop shot; (c) drive, etc. (Fig. 31).

4. When the set routines of (3) above are mastered, each shot should again be practised so as to give greater variety of feeding and reply: (a) B may now feed to centre, forehand, and backhand as he wishes; or (b) A may similarly play his shots straight or cross-court as he wishes; or (c) the last two exercises

113

may be combined. To ensure continuity of feeding, the additional feeder, C, should be brought in. Return of service and return of smash may be practised as well as other strokes.

5. A further progression is for the striker to play two or more different shots consecutively. (a) A clears straight; B drops cross-court: A lobs cross-court; B clears straight, etc. (b) A clears backhanded, straight; B drops cross-court. A lobs straight,

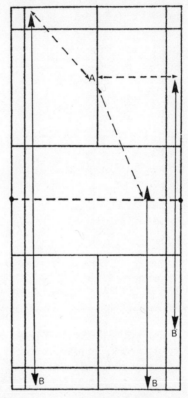

Fig. 31. Rallying and footwork: A plays clears or lobs or backhand drives to feeder B; A moves back to base between each shot.

forehanded; C smashes cross-court: A lob returns, straight; B clears, straight, etc.

6. A fourth player can be brought in as an additional striker, or, on occasions, feeder. Complementary shots may then be practised in sequence. (a) Partners A and B drop straight to C and D respectively, who respectively feed B and A with

114

cross-court lobs. Similarly, with clears, smashes, drives, etc. Or (b) A serves high to C; C smashes at B, straight; B plays push return, straight; D dabs down at net.

7. After these routines have been practised, conditioned games should be played. These, by their very conditions, ensure rapid repetition of one or more strokes, or of a particular tactic, e.g. (a) no lifting in mixed; (b) only drops and attacking clears as overhead shots to be used in men's; (c) all serves to be flicks or drives; (d) bonus points for net interceptions or drive returns of smash.

8. Finally, normal games of 8 or 11 up should be played in which players concentrate on using strokes or tactics just practised, as often as it is wise to do so.

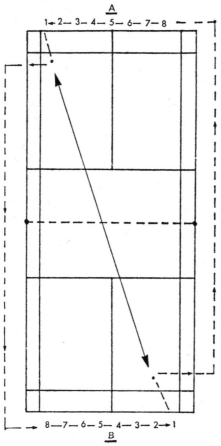

Fig. 32. Running round game 1.

RUNNING ROUND GAMES

1. Two teams, A and B, each stand behind a base line. No. 1 of A hits high serve to No. 1 of B who in turn clears to No. 2 of A who clears to No. 2 of B, and so on. Each player after his shot sets off to circle the court anti-clockwise, playing another clear from the opposite end. Playing and running is continuous. Failure to hit shuttle or to hit it a certain length leads to loss of a life. After three such losses, player drops out

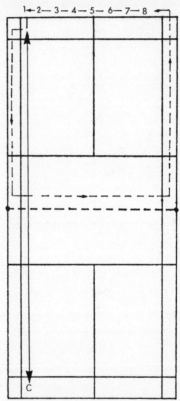

Fig. 33. Running round game 2.

and running speeds up (Fig. 32). Beware post guy-lines!

2. Ten or twelve players line up along one base line. Coach, playing down the side line, feeds each player in turn. When the player has played either a clear, a drop or a smash, he runs forward to the net, chassés along its length, and then runs backwards to the base line to rejoin the group (Fig. 33).

3. As in (2) above, but six players stand behind right-hand court only on each side of the net. Coach or competent feeders stand in left-hand courts, one opposite each group. The latter feed for the chosen shot straight down the side lines. Players run as above but round their own half-court only (Fig. 34).

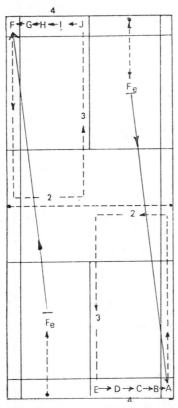

Fig. 34. Clearing and footwork practice: A, B, C, D and E clear in turn to Fe. Each then (1) runs to net; (2) *chassés* across it; (3) runs backwards; (4) *chassés* back to position; F, G, H, I and J do likewise.

4. As in (1) above, but players, hitting the shuttle in turn, feed one another before running up to the net, chasséing along it, and running backwards to rejoin their group.

5. Six-a-side singles. Six players stand behind each base line. One player from each side takes up position on court and a normal game of singles is started. Each player plays one stroke only before moving off court as quickly as possible in any

117

direction to rejoin his team. Following player may position himself on court as preceding player plays his shot. Game may be played at first just to get long rallies; later, it can be played all out to win points.

6. As in (5) but all players stand behind base line and coach alone, on the opposite side, makes returns (5 consecutive returns by players count as a point to them).

7. Six-a-side doubles. One pair from each team of six plays initial rally. Losers of this and subsequent rallies are replaced by next pair.

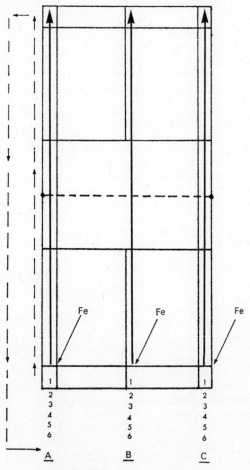

Fig. 35. Elementary group practices.

GROUP PRACTICES

1. Three teams line up in file behind base line. Feeder, mid-court, in front of each team, feeds by hand for clear. Each player in file plays a clear, runs to retrieve shuttle and bring it back to feeder before rejoining his file. Targets should be marked on floor and scores kept. Running must be carefully organized or chaos will result. This exercise (Fig. 35) can also be used for smash, drop, drive, and high serve (no feeder).

2. Four teams, in file, one behind each corner of court. After initial high serve by first player in team A, first player in team B, directly opposite, clears. Each player then clears in turn, all quickly moving off court to rejoin file. Teams C and D play similarly down the other side line.

3. As in (2), but one team plays half-smashes, the other makes lofted return; or one team drops; the other makes a lob return.

4. A team is spaced along each front service line. Team A serves to targets and counts number of attempts made before all players have hit their targets three times. Team B act as fags before, in their turn, trying to better A's score. This practice can also be used for flick and for high serves.

5. Coach feeds each player in team opposite him in turn with a high shot (serve, clear or lob). As he plays his shot, he calls to striker which shot (drop, smash or clear) the latter is to play.

6. As in (5), the student plays whichever shot he chooses.

RACQUET MANOEUVRABILITY

1. See practices under 'Grip' (page 46) and 'Rallying Against Wall' (page 111).

2. A stands at net to dab shuttle down to B, standing opposite him about mid-court. B returns shuttle to A with underhand shot. Pace of hit and return is steadily increased. Later, shots are played alternately, backhand and forehand, by B and/or A. Five or six pairs can play at once across width of hall.

3. A and B stand opposite each other, both about 14ft from the net. They drive fast to each other. Gradually, moving in, they may squat lower and lower, pushing the shuttle at each other.

4. A stands mid-court; B and C stand on opposite front service line pushing a succession of shots at ever-increasing speed into his body or just to each side of it.

119

MISCELLANEOUS PRACTICES

1. Golf. One or two players. Targets are placed in each of the four corners of both doubles service courts on one side of the net; one target is also set for a singles serve. Player serves to each target in turn, counting number of strokes needed to hit all nine targets. If a pair plays, each player serves in turn, counting either strokes or 'holes' as in golf.

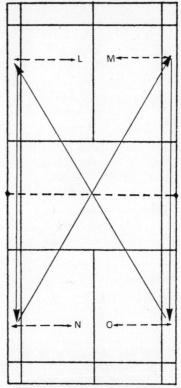

Fig. 36. Pattern driving.

2. Pattern Driving. Four players: one mid-court in each half-court. L drives straight to N's backhand; N drives backhand cross-court to L's partner, M; M drives backhand straight to N's partner, O; O drives forehand cross-court to L. After each stroke, player should move towards centre line so that his next stroke is not cramped. At intervals, players move round one position so that they then practise all variations of drive (Fig. 36).

120

3. The same pattern is used as in (2) above but the strokes may be varied. (a) All players play clears, forehand and backhand; (b) L and M initially play drops which N and O return with lobs; (c) L and M initially play smashes which N and O answer with lofted returns.

4. Interception. As in (2) above, but a net player is brought in on each side to attempt interception. Those playing drives can either keep to the pattern given above, varying it just occasionally to prevent too obvious anticipation, or alter the pattern completely although still hitting to the side lines.

5. Net Singles. Two players take up position as net players. Using full width of court, they play a rally of net shots all of which must be taken just below the tape and hit upwards.

6. As in (5), but after initial shots by each player the shuttle may be hit down; it must, however, land within a line drawn parallel to the net and 10ft from it.

7. Simple Single. A plays a normal single, except that he must hit every shot to B who stands all the time in one corner of the court. A weaker player can thus give a much better one long rallies and the practice of being able to play shots from any part of his court to a small target area in the other. B should vary his position from time to time so that A can employ a full range of strokes.

AGILITY PRACTICES : see pages 135–137. PRESSURE TRAINING PRACTICES : see page 133. ACCURACY AND CONSISTENCY PRACTICES : see page 150. DECEPTION PRACTICES : see page 153. CONDITIONED GAMES : see page 122.

12

CONDITIONED GAMES

These games are played normally except for some rules laid down by the coach to ensure frequent repetition of a particular stroke(s) or tactic(s) in match conditions. Conditioned games are much used in coaching other sports. I have devised a number of such games to suit varied needs. They have these advantages:

1. They avoid the sterility of formal stroke practice in pairs.

2. They are an excellent means of instilling tactics by repetitive practice without a laboured build-up.

3. They are specific, competitive, novel, varied, capable of progression and therefore interesting.

4. By pinpointing one stroke or idea, they give the player time to think and experiment.

A simple example is men's or ladies' doubles played normally except for one condition: all serves must be high. What results?

STROKE PRODUCTION

1. A practises high serves (varying placements and trajectories).

2. C practises smashing (varying pace, placement steepness).

3. A and B practise one or more returns of smash.

4. D practises net interceptions.

TACTICS

1. A and B learn to take up slightly varying defensive positions according to placement of service and to seek always to turn defence into attack.

2. C and D learn to take up back and front position for attack, and strive always to maintain that attack.

3. C learns to smash for his partner.

4. D practises net interceptions and, if his partner is slow across court, comes back to intercept attacking lobs to opposite corner.

Not bad for one practice! (Should be taken step by step.)

In such a game it is often best for A to serve a dozen consecutive serves to C before D (and then A and B) have their turns at smashing: each player thus moves on to a new skill after he has had repeated practice at another. If enthusiasm flags, a score (a point a rally) can be kept.

To save time still further (and irrelevant strokes) a rally may be restricted to the first half dozen or so strokes. Then: (1) Whichever side is attacking (hitting down) takes the point, or, (2) the defenders win the point because the attackers, from an initial advantage, have failed to win the rally, or, (3) defenders take the point the first time attackers 'lift' instead of hitting down.

These methods are particularly useful in serve, return of serve, return of return of serve, and return of return of return of serve practices, the basic aim of which can otherwise be lost in the subsequent rallies.

A few conditioned games are suggested below. Devise others to suit your students' own particular needs. Insist that all students play intelligently to gain full benefit from the practice and not merely to score early winners by taking advantage of their pre-knowledge of the shot to be played. Occasional variants (e.g. low serve instead of high, or fast clear instead of drop shot) may be allowed so that situations are not too cut and dried.

SINGLES

1. All low serves.
2. To achieve length: all high serves, clears or drops falling between front and back doubles service line are 'left' and count as point lost.
3. Add to (2), all smashes must land between side line and a line drawn parallel to and 12-18 inches from it (Fig. 37).

MIXED

1. To encourage use of full width of court: all shots landing between doubles and singles side lines (a) earn bonus point whether striker or partner served, or (b) are the *only* winning shots.
2. To condition lady to dealing with high serve and subsequent net shot: all serves to her are high or flick and return of her shot must be played to the net.
3. No lobbing or clearing allowed.

MEN'S OR LADIES' DOUBLES

To teach basic tactics all rallies start with singles high serve to *base* line, then:

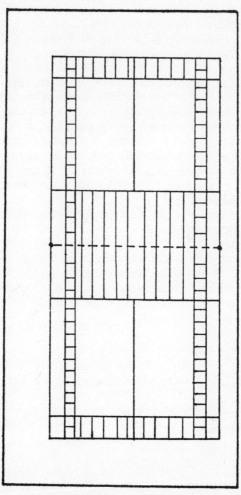

Fig. 37. Restricted singles: Only shots falling in shaded areas are 'good'.

1. Receiver plays drops only: defenders lob.
2. Receiver plays drops or fast clears: defenders lob or clear.
3. Receiver plays drops or fast clears: defender-play lobs, upward net shots, or clears; receiver's partner plays net shots.
4. Receiver plays drops or fast clears: defenders play lob, upwards or downwards net shot, or clears.
5. Receiver plays drops or fast clears and smashes when they

124

elicit short replies: defenders play lobs, net shots, clears, or any return of smash.

Similar progressive practices can be built up for (a) smash and return (b) low (or flick) serves and returns.

GENERAL QUALITIES

1. CONSISTENCY

(a) Coach 'calls' careless or unforced errors: opponent(s) given a bonus point whether serving or not (play 21 up).

(b) Three players a side: two on court. When one player makes an unforced error, the third replaces him. This procedure continues, at each unforced error, throughout the game. Normal scoring and/or each player counts the highest number of consecutive rallies for which he stayed on court.

2. DETERMINATION

Game starts with one player or side 5-12 down to the other. The object is to encourage the side starting at 5 to fight back to win the game and the side starting at 12 to win quickly without losing concentration. Offer extra games as incentives.

3. CONCENTRATION

(a) Each game consists of three points only.

(b) Each game consists of seven points only but for the first point score 5; second point, 6; third point, 7; fourth point, 8; fifth point, 9; sixth point, 10; and seventh, 15.

Both (a) and (b) encourage players to fight for every point.

4. SPEED

Coach awards point only when rally is won by speed of movement or by anticipation; play 5 up or game may be lengthy.

5. DECEPTION

Coach awards bonus point whenever final opening is made or rally is won by a shot played deceptively.

6. CONSISTENCY AND STAMINA

Both players or sides play only clears; or drops, clears and lobs, within ever narrower limits.

13

PHYSICAL FITNESS

TRAINING

Fitness is the capacity of an individual to perform work. In badminton, this means the ability to undergo the longest periods of physical and mental stress and strain at full stretch or top performance, and the ability quickly to regain peak condition after the shortest of rests. So often when skill is equal, it is in the last points of the third set that the fitter player surges into the lead and on to victory. When stamina wanes, so does skill. In modern play, fitness is an essential that ranks as high as techniques or tactics.

It cannot be fully and economically achieved or scientifically measured merely by playing badminton. Fitness embraces stamina, strength, speed, power, mobility and skill. All these can be attained by a combination of running, weight training, circuits and pressure exercises.

FUNDAMENTALS

Whichever method is adopted as best fitted for the individual, temperamentally and physically, and the local conditions, the following general points will apply.

The form adopted must be specific, i.e. it must simulate as far as humanly possible the conditions pertaining to the game itself; it must have common elements. It has been proved that there is very little carry over of benefit from one form of training to another, or from one form of sport to another. One hour's hard training, provided both coach and student apply themselves intelligently throughout, is worth two hours of sporadic and careless work. The will to continue this hard and gruelling work is better maintained if it is made enjoyable. To this end, competition should be introduced, and training done in friendly groups, with parents or less energetic friends as audience. Exercising to music results in increased productivity.

Whatever method is adopted, a not too strenuous start is advised. This applies particularly to younger and older players who may let enthusiasm outrun discretion. Once a basic fitness has been achieved, then a player must specialize. By overload and progressions, he will seek maximum fitness. In this training, it is essential to be regular, to avoid 'missed' days. Once fitness has been achieved pre-season, reduced but regular training will maintain that fitness; but if training is entirely neglected fitness will be lost just as fast as it was built up.

Training as far as possible must be organized to suit the individual. Above all regular testing and recording must be carried out: this shows not only the success or failure of the training scheme but it also supplies essential motivation.

RUNNING
This is an excellent means of building up stamina and cardio-vascular fitness. It can take a variety of forms.

JOGGING
In this the knees are scarcely lifted so the feet just skim the ground. It is useful for warming up or as a first step for the unfit. (A mile should take 8 to 10 minutes.)

FARTLEK
This is sprinting, running, jogging and striding over different types of country, i.e. road, grass, hills, beach, sand dunes.

REPETITION RUNNING
For speed, 50 or 75 yards are run flat out an ever-increasing number of times but several minutes' rest is allowed between runs to ensure cardio-vascular recovery.

RESISTANCE RUNNING
This is running up sand, snow or scree.

INTERVAL RUNNING
Sprinting is followed by complete rest, walking or, ideally, jogging. Economical of time, it nevertheless best adapts the body to cope with the oxygen debt. Progressions are easily obtained by varying distances and times; the form and length of 'rest'; and the number of repetitions.

For badminton, the best method is to jog 30 yards, sprint 30 yards, jog 30 yards and so on. It may incorporate running backwards or zig-zagging. After 2 minutes of this the pulse rate should be up to 140-180. With reasonable fitness it should drop to 120 after 90 seconds 'rest' when the stint can be repeated. Five minutes of a gentle version of this, with arm movements, after a hard game or practice session, helps a player to recuperate by diffusing fatigue products.

WEIGHT TRAINING

This is doing exercises with weights; it is not weight-lifting. By pitting muscles against ever-increasing resistances, each of the thousands of individual fibres is thickened, and so strengthened. As a result strength, agility, speed, power, general endurance and the cardio-vascular system are all improved. Such improvement can be accurately measured.

It is vital to warm up and to warm down before and after these exercises. Each exercise must first be practised to ensure correct technique and safety. The weight used initially is that with which the exercise can just be completed 10 times; this is often between two-thirds and three-quarters of the maximum weight the performer can use for one repetition.

In actual training, try to increase the ten repetitions by two or three each session. For badminton, in which activity is seldom sustained for longer than 60 seconds, a target of twenty repetitions with this initial weight is fixed. When this is achieved, the new ten repetition maximum weight is ascertained and used until again twenty repetitions can be performed.

In the early weeks of training, exercises should be done two or three times a week. Once a real basic fitness has been attained, exercises once a week will sustain it. Since badminton players need power rather than strength, the accent may, at first, be on fewer but fast repetitions with heavy weights for strength; then, pre-season on more repetitions but with lighter weights at speed for power.

Weight training can take varied forms, but since such exercises must be specific, these were specially worked out for me by bio-mechanical analysis and with an electro-micrograph to ascertain just which muscles are most used in badminton strokes. For them, I am much indebted to that enthusiast Dr Peter Travers, AAA Coach for England teams, and lecturer at St Luke's College, Exeter.

To build up a weight-training circuit, one or two exercises should be chosen from each anatomical group. Care should be taken that consecutive exercises do not use the same basic muscle groups.

128

48

LADIES' DOUBLES

48 World Champions in action: Margaret Allen follows through and recovers quickly after powerful straight smash; Sue Whetnall, racquet raised, on toes, alert, is on T-junction ready to intercept net return or flat push

49

MIXED

49 Ray Sharp tempts left-handed Margaret Allen and draws her partner, Paul Whetnall, across with a well-concealed half-court push

50 Sue Whetnall has quickly come across to intercept, backhanded, Paul's probing half-court return; Margaret seeks to cover it

51 Paul has smashed cross-court; Sue has intercepted whilst Ray has covered the likely straight smash; Margaret drops back desperately to retrieve

50

51

52

COACHING

52 Shadowing: group (including future world champion) shadow overhead clear as the Author moves among them to make corrections. (NB: Left-handers on left of group.)

53 Twelve to a Court: each of three groups, staggered for safety, consists of server, smasher, defender and net player practising routine sequence of shots

54 Demonstration: Warwick Shute (former English international, and National Coach) keeps Notts group absorbed with a fluent demonstration spiced with humour in Lilleshall's fine sports hall

53

54

55 Practice: Twelve on a court; six practice low serve or net shots; six play rallies of clears

56 Manual guidance: Peter Roper gives PE Teacher, Anne Smith, kinaesthetic feel of backhand drive

57 Twelve keen juniors on one court; six give accurate hand feeding; six play clear (or drop, or smash)

58 Twenty-four to a court practise clear; staggered centre line feed strikers for clear to opposite wall (Plenty of shuttles needed)

59 And to cap the lot – veteran Author takes off in jumping smash!

Breathing should be inhaling through the mouth as effort is made and exhaling as weights are returned to starting position. To avoid dizziness or even black-outs, remember that in squats and pullovers that effort is made in the second movement, not the first.

EXERCISES FOR THE LEGS

Squat jumps Go down into no more than a quarter squat and then jump as high as possible into the air. The leg must be fully extended and the 'drive' comes from the extension of the hip, knee, ankle and toes. Bend the knees on landing.

Heel Raising with the Toes on a Step Stand with the toes on a small step so that the heels can drop lower than the toes. Rise on the toes as high as possible and then lower the heels.

Step-ups on to a Bench Stand facing a bench. Place one foot on the bench and step up so that both feet are on the bench and the knees are quite straight. Then step down again with the same foot leading. Repeat with alternate feet.

Knee Extensions (This exercise should always be included in any circuit as it is vital for springing.) Sit on a high box with the knees supported and the lower leg hanging down vertically. The weight is attached to the foot. Straighten the knee fully so that the whole leg is held horizontally. Then slowly relax. It is essential that the knee is *fully* extended in this exercise.

EXERCISES FOR THE BACK AND TRUNK

Back Extensions with Twist Lie on a high box on your face. The legs must be fixed by a partner. Allow the trunk to hang down over the end of the box. With the hands behind the neck, extend the spine as fully as possible. The weight is held behind the neck. Relax and allow the trunk to flex forward, then repeat but this time as you extend and raise the trunk, twist to the right. Repeat straight back and then repeat with a twist to the left.

Abdominal Curls with Twist Lie on a high box on your back. The legs must be fixed by a partner. Allow the trunk to hyper-extend over the end of the box. With the hands behind the neck, curl up to bring the head down to the knees. The weight is held behind the neck. Repeat with a twist to the right bringing the left elbow down outside the right knee. Repeat straight and then with twist to left.

NB. In these exercises each set of four should be repeated three times to start with.

129

Straight Arm Pullovers   Lie on a bench on your back. Grasp a weight on a short bar with your hands. Extend the arms over the head as far back as possible, keeping the arms straight and the small of the back firmly pressed against the bench. Bring the arms down to the starting position and repeat.

Bent Arm Pullovers   Grasp weight as for previous exercise. Extend arms over the head and then bend the elbows, straighten elbows and recover.

Behind the Neck Press   Either place bar on a stand and then lift it onto the shoulders, or 'clean' the bar to shoulder level and lift it over the head on to the shoulders. Keeping the elbows well back in the plane of the bar, straighten the arms and lift the bar over the head as high as possible. Lower on to shoulders and repeat.

Elbow Extensions   Using dumb-bells. Extend the arms vertically above the head. Bend the elbows alternately allowing the weight to come down behind the neck. Extend the arm again fully.

Shoulder Extensions   Lie on your face on a high box. Grasp a dumb-bell in each hand. Allow the arms to hang down vertically. Extend the arms alternately backwards, getting as full backwards extension of the shoulder as possible.

Bench Press   Lie on your back on a bench. Have a partner give you a barbell which you grip at shoulder width with the bar lying across your chest. Push the bar upwards and straighten your arms. IT IS ESSENTIAL THAT A PARTNER IS READY TO TAKE THE BAR FROM YOU AT ANY INSTANT DURING THIS EXERCISE.

EXERCISES FOR THE WRISTS

Hold a dumb-bell in each hand with the forearms horizontal and the palms facing downwards. Cock the wrist backwards as far as possible.

Repeat the above exercise with the palms facing upwards.

CIRCUIT TRAINING

This is another popular and efficient way of achieving basic fitness, strength and local muscle endurance, and improved cardiovascular action. A sequence of simple strengthening and endurance exercises is devised to suit the individual and his training facilities, and to exercise all main or specific muscle groups.

First each exercise must be correctly learnt. Then the performer does as many repetitions as he can of each exercise in 30 (or in 60) seconds. He rests for a minute between each exercise. This number of test repetitions is divided by a half or two-thirds. The resultant figure will be the number of repetitions done in actual training.

Thus, when training starts, the necessary apparatus is set out. The performer does each of his six or eight exercises for the agreed number of repetitions, and in such order that adjacent muscle groups are never worked consecutively. There is no rest between exercises; only when the whole circuit has been completed. Such recovery period should be kept to a minimum and not exceed one minute. Three circuits are performed and the time taken noted.

For progression, the performer now increases the number of repetitions or the difficulty of the exercise (increased weights, etc.) whilst still attempting to complete the three circuits in the same time as previously.

A different method of progression is this: the performer's total time for the circuit, once well learnt, is noted. Let us say this is 18 minutes. This number is reduced by one-third to find the target time. The performer, as he improves, aims to reduce his time eventually to $18 \times \frac{2}{3} = 12$ minutes. When he achieves this, progression is by increased repetitions or difficulty. A new target time is worked out and aimed for. For variety, a completely different circuit may be devised. Time needed should not exceed 20 minutes.

AT HOME

1. Step-ups (leg). On to bench 20 inches high, or a chair.

2. Press-ups (arms). Later with feet on chair (women do press-ups from knees).

3. Trunk Curls (abdominals). Hands slide to knees only.

4. Wrist Twist (wrist). Rolling and unrolling weight tied on to stick.

5. Single Leg Over (laterals). On back, palms down, arms outstretched. Alternately raise legs to *perpendicular* then lower to touch opposite hand.

6. Tuck jumps (explosive power). Standing: two skip jumps, then jump high, bringing knees to chest.

7. Dorsal Raise (back). Face down; arms outstretched; raise legs and arms simultaneously.

8. Running. With back against wall.

131

| | Repetitions | | |
In the Gym	Fair	Good	Very Good
1. Curl Sit-ups (abdomen). Weight held behind neck	12	18	25
2. Bench Jumps (legs). With dumb-bells	12	15	20
3. Jump Chins (arms)	8	10	12
4. Dorsal Lift, 10 lbs (back)	5	7	9
5. Squats (legs). With dumb-bells or barbells	12	16	20
6. Rope Climb (arms)	1	2	3
7. Wrist Rolling (wrist). Barbell and disc	3	4	5
8. Shuttle Run (stamina). 10 × 10 yards	1	2	3

CIRCUIT TRAINING TO MUSIC

As the beat of the tribal tom-tom rouses one to war so the beat of the latest 'pop' instrumental record can 'send' not only its devotees but also players in training. This marked rhythm acts on a part of the brain – the thalamus – which sorts out sensory perceptions. As a result, a semi-hypnotic state is created in which inhibitions are lost and more work can be done, more enjoyably, sometimes without realization of effort or fatigue.

CIRCUIT TRAINING

Exercises are first taught, and then practised to music. Work begins and ends on the first and last notes of the taped music. This should be recorded with music for exercise and recovery periods carefully timed.

Press-ups (arms)
Hopping (legs)
Curls with twist (abdomen)
Stick-body (back)
Side-lying with legs scissoring

Jump Chins (arms)
Continuous Spring Jumps (legs)
Sitting Tucks (abdomen)
Empty Wheelbarrow (back)
Shuttle-running (stamina)

It should be preceded by warming-up running to music.

INTERVAL TRAINING

Tapes in this case are prepared with a continuous run of music with different rhythms. The rhythms are chosen to suit all paces (jogging, striding, running); the timings to suit the fitness of a particular group. Performers run in time with the music or vary running by hopping, skip-jumping, split-jumping, or running with high knee lift or with straight legs.

An excellent circuit for performing to music is as follows:

PRESSURE TRAINING

This is a way of improving both speed of reaction and local muscle endurance by playing badminton. It is only for the player who is already 'grooved' in stroke production. He plays a stroke (or strokes) at high speed for ever longer periods until fatigue causes loss of co-ordination; he is thus fitted to play well the longest and toughest of rallies (Fig. 38).

EXAMPLES

1. Student plays succession of clears; between each shot he advances as near as he can to the *front* service line. (Similarly with drop shots and conversely with lobs.)

2. Student plays drop shot, feed plays net shot; student plays return net shot, feed lobs; student plays drop, and so on. Vary by playing two or three net shots before lobbing, or vice versa. Hand feeding may also be used.

3. Feeder, with twenty shuttles in hand and on a chair, hits shuttles at different heights to different parts of court; student smashes to one or all of three targets set on side and centre lines, without respite.

4. Student and feed hit high serves to each other simultaneously; each clears straight to the other, keeping two shuttles in flight at once.

5. Student smashes and immediately follows in, to (a) kill push return at net or (b) play net return and then run back to smash feeder's lob, and so into net again.

6. Two players side by side (or coach, by hand), feed student who plays as man in mixed; his returns may be any shot except net shots. Each feeder holds three or four shuttles, hitting another to student as soon as rally breaks down, to allow him no respite. Similarly, for a net player.

7. Student plays singles against two opponents: he plays his shots as though player making last stroke was only opponent. Feeds take shuttle early and keep rally going. (Feeds may play sides or back and front.)

8. Two feeds pressurize (except for occasional shot to forehand) student's backhand. Latter must go to centre court base between shots.

9. Student smashes from base line at two defenders who lob repeatedly.

10. Two feeders push or drive fast shots into student's body.

11. B and C (with ten shuttles each) alternately feed D and E who smash at A whilst F intercepts at net.

12. Student smashes from normal position to nominated side of two defenders. Latter play push or net returns. Student comes and plays net return. Defenders lob; student goes back to smash.

133

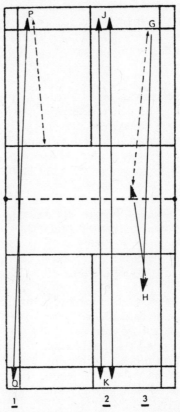

Fig. 38. Pressure training: (1) P clears to Q and runs in to front service line between each shot. (2) J and K clear simultaneously to each other with two shuttles. (3) G smashes and then runs in to take H's net return as early as possible.

In all cases feeders play not to win but to keep student constantly on the move seeking to return difficult but possible shots. They should allow little respite between rallies. Student must still strive for accuracy and consistency, as must feeder(s).

MOBILITY

DYNAMIC
This is rapid repetition of a precisely done body movement, e.g. with back to and 2ft from wall, stand erect; squat to touch floor between feet with flat hands; stand up, turning to right and touch wall with flat hands; squat as before and repeat to the left. Count repetitions in 15 seconds.

134

Full range of movement at the joints gives these advantages: (a) greater power and efficiency; (b) increased reach; (c) better co-ordination; (d) reduced likelihood of muscle injuries.

The following exercises should be slow, strong, controlled movements. The joint is moved to its limit then additional movement is sought by muscular effort. Joints should be mobile in all directions. Precede these exercises by jogging and warming-up.

SPINE

With legs astride and arms horizontal, twist as far as possible to left, then smoothly to the right, and so on.

SHOULDER

Standing, feet astride. Raise arms to 45°. Without bending elbows, press arms back as far as possible. Repeat with arms at 90°, 135°, 180°.

UPPER TRUNK

Prone lying, star position. Lift left arm backwards and downwards as far as possible. Recover and repeat with right arm, etc.

HAMSTRING

Raise left leg horizontal and so foot is fixed at hip-height. Reach forward to touch toes eight times, then change to opposite leg.

ANKLE

Sit on floor, legs outstretched, heels and big toes pressed together throughout. (a) Press feet forward, then backward; (b) Turn soles in, then out.

AGILITY

From improved mobility may spring greater agility. On a small badminton court, agility is more necessary than sheer speed. Balance is an integral part of agility so it must become automatic to keep the centre of gravity as low as possible and between the feet. This plays a main part in stopping and changing direction. Skipping, and the following exercises, can do much to speed up footwork (Fig. 39).

1. Place a shuttle on each side line. Stand on centre line holding another shuttle. Move to right; pick up shuttle on side line, replacing it with the shuttle held. Move to left, doing as before. Continue, using badminton footwork, and count number of times right side line is reached in 60, 90 or 120 seconds.

2. Feeder stands on chair just behind base line. Player runs forward to pick up shuttle placed 2ft from net; he runs backwards and in 'shadowing' the clear, hands shuttle to feeder. The latter has meantime thrown another shuttle to replace the first one. Each picking up of shuttle counts one.

3. Players stand 3yds from doubles side line. On 'Go' they run forward to it, stop and run backwards to start; they then run to singles line and back; and similarly to the other three lines. (Repeat five times.) If the net is removed, this may also be done down the length of the court, using the service lines.

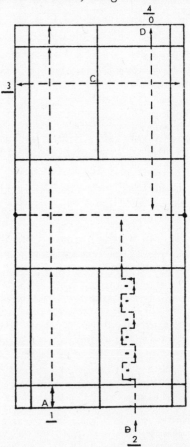

Fig. 39. Agility exercises: (1) A runs up to and back from each line (Ex. 3). (2) B does maze run (Ex. 4). (3) C does shuttle run across court (Ex. 1). (4) D does shuttle run up and down half-court (Ex. 2). (*Not* all at the same time!)

136

4. Place six chairs or poles in a staggered line (distance apart may be varied from 2ft to 6ft). Player starts 10ft from first chair, runs up to it and weaves through others to touch line 10ft in front of last chair; from this mark he runs backwards through chairs in reverse direction to starting line.

5. Player (a) jumps on and off box horse (about 4ft high); (b) weaves round three footballs (5ft apart); (c) *jumps* over four hurdles (about 3ft 6in high and 3ft apart); (d) weaves through four staggered poles (3ft apart); (e) does five shuttle runs (10ft each), before sprinting back to start. Course may be covered two, three or four times consecutively. Times should be recorded and individual or team relay races run. The course can easily be varied.

6. Two players with one tennis ball stand 10-12ft apart. One bounces the ball; the other has to catch it before it hits the floor a second time. The latter then instantly bounces it similarly for his partner. Deception may be employed and each player tries to extend his partner to utmost without breaking the rally. Pressure must be maintained until one player cries 'Enough'.

7. Player goes on court and plays 'shadow' rallies against an imaginary opponent. He varies length of rallies, speed of movement and brings in much turning and stopping.

TESTING

This is essential for motivation and for proving the success of training schedule.

FLEXIBILITY OF JOINTS
Use a goniometer (two hinged arms fixed to a protractor) for extent, and an elgon for dynamic flexibility.

STRENGTH
Use a dynamometer (rather akin to a spring balance!). If unobtainable count number of 'chins' or 'press-ups' done.

SPEED
Use stop-watch timing for straight runs over a measured distance.

AGILITY
Use and time Exercises 1 and 2 in 'Agility'.

STAMINA
Harvard Step Test Student steps up to full height on to 20 inch high platform every 2 seconds for 5 minutes (i.e. 150 times). Pulse rate is taken (a) $1-1\frac{1}{2}$ minutes; (b) $2-2\frac{1}{2}$ minutes; (c)

3-3½ minutes after completion of exercise. These counts added together and then divided into 15,000 give Fitness Index (below 75, Poor; 75-80, Fair; 81-88 Average; 89-95, Good; 96-110, Very Good).

POWER

Sargent Jump Test First, stand with heels flat on ground and mark on wall highest point that can be reached. Then, after a few arm swings, jump vertically to touch wall as high as possible. Measure height jumped vertically each time in the best of three tries. (Poor: below 18.5 inches; Average: 19.5-20.4 inches; Good: 20.5-21.4 inches; Very Good: 21.5-23 inches.)

Standing Broad Jump Stand with feet level but slightly apart. Bend knees and swing arms forwards and backwards whilst rising and falling, on balls of feet, then leap forward as far as possible. After practice jumps, measure best of three consecutive jumps.

GENERAL HEALTH

DIET

This is the province of the specialist dietician so let it suffice to make these brief points. Food is a player's energy fuel.

This energy is largely produced by the oxidation of carbohydrates (cereals, potatoes, starches, sugar) and fats. The former possess the advantage of producing more energy per litre of oxygen than the latter and being more easily digestible and assimilable. On the other hand, fat makes a better long-term store of energy than carbohydrates. Protein (meat, fish, cheese and eggs), containing vital amino acids, is needed for body building and maintenance. These should be in the proportions of 4:1:1. Vitamins in recognized quantities are essential for general health; overdoses are not only ineffective but in the cases of A and D, actually deleterious.

A player in hard training or during tournaments will need to consume a diet well balanced in the above items to replace the 4,000-5,000 calories that he will burn up. The following are the calories in each ounce of the food named: plain biscuits (107), white bread (73), potatoes (21), sugar (108), jam (71), chocolate (160), steamed pudding (100), butter (211), milk (17), cheese (117), eggs (45), fish (55), bacon (128), chicken (38), greens (7-9), orange (10), banana (21), dates (68). Calories absorbed in food and not consumed by exercise turn to fat.

Moderate sized meals of a familiar, easily digestible type

138

should be eaten at regular hours. They should be taken, well salted, 2-3 hours before a match; thereafter light high-calorific snacks or glucose and salt drinks should be the order of the day. Meals should be varied, tasty, and can be served hot or cold. It well repays the effort to ask an expert to make out a diet to suit the individual.

SMOKING
Apart from long-term consideration, it should be taboo because it narrows blood vessels and air passages, so restricting the energizing of muscles and easy breathing.

RECREATION
To overcome mental staleness the player should be encouraged to have a wide range of interests and, though dedicated, not become single-track minded.

SLEEP
The amount needed for body and mind to rest from training stresses varies according to a player's age and temperament. Most people need 8 hours' sleep, at regular times, as early as possible. Television, books or music may help secure relaxation before going to bed; it is fatally easy to lie awake for hours replaying practice sessions or matches. A warm bed, light bedclothes, open windows and drawn curtains, and a warm drink, will help promote easy and deep sleep. Its value is too frequently underestimated.

MINOR INJURIES

No one man is likely to be a doctor, physio-therapist, masseur and coach all rolled into one. However, a little commonsense knowledge on medical matters may alleviate suffering or possibility of greater injury. If in any doubt, consult the expert.

CRAMP
Prevention is better than cure – by which time a game may have been lost. Salt as well as water is lost in the cooling process, sweating. Lack of the former may lead to cramp, of the latter, to stress on the cardio-vascular system. A drink (half a teaspoonful of salt and glucose to a pint of water and lemon juice) should be drunk before a strenuous game and even – in small sips – during it.

If a player does get cramp, he should force his toes up and back towards his legs so as to stretch the affected muscle group.

139

STITCH

It is best cured by (a) sitting on the ground and squeezing bent knees tightly into the chest; (b) standing up and stretching the arms straight overhead; (c) repeatedly touching the toes, with the knees straight.

MUSCLE SORENESS

This is best overcome by rubbing liniment or embrocation *gently* into the affected muscles.

PULLED OR TORN MUSCLES

This is a tearing of the muscle fibre, caused by overwork or awkward movements; it prevents full play of the muscles. The slight bleeding between or within the muscles causes a swelling and adhesions.

Do not rub leg, so causing damage to further fibres, but pack ice or tie a cold, wet towel round to stop bleeding. Tie a crepe bandage firmly round the injured limb and raise it above heart level. Keep it still for a day and then gently exercise it. Warmth (hot water-bottle or short-wave diathermy) is then helpful.

COLDS

Little can be done once a cold is caught. So seek to prevent them by seeing that players eat and sleep well, get plenty of fresh air, avoid those with colds, and keep warm after games by immediately donning a track-suit, then showering and changing.

MASSAGE

On the whole, kneading massage may do more harm than good in treating pulled muscles as it merely increases haemorrhage or disrupts more fibres. It and friction massage are, however, excellent as a temporary revivifier. Three minutes massage can bring about a 70% recovery. Legs should be massaged simultaneously. This eliminates 'stopping substances' such as potassium, which lower contractile strength. Repeated massage can, however, exhaust the muscle fuel reservoirs.

14

MENTAL APPROACH

No matter how fit or how skilled in stroke production the student is, it will avail him little if he has not an equally sound mental approach. The coach, therefore, must not give mere lip service to the following points but should incorporate them in building up a routine and practices for matches and tournaments.

PRE-MATCH PREPARATION

CHECKING-UP

This starts long before the player even reaches the hall. Heavy, fatty, indigestible food or fizzy drinks are avoided. Early arrival is assured by exact knowledge of the whereabouts of the hall, and of train or bus times. Clothing and accessories are checked: zips, buttons, laces, straps, sweat-bands, glucose, salt tablets, spectacle de-mister, talc, etc. If possible, personal and business cares are set aside.

CHARTING THE HALL

After changing unhurriedly, the player should carefully study the problems that every new hall holds.

FLOOR

A slippery floor demands rough soled shoes or an application of light paraffin oil at intervals to the soles. Tactics may have to be varied: the opponent must be made to run as much as possible and more deception than usual employed. The student himself must anticipate thoughtfully to avoid having to rush to shots which will make quick recovery difficult.

HEAT

If the hall is very hot, a salt, water, lemon and glucose mixture should be available for small drinks. Spectacles should be de-misted, sweat-pads worn, or a small towel hung from the pocket, and hands talced. Also it should be remembered that the shuttle will fly faster.

LIGHTS

The player should always watch a game (though not a tense one that affects him) immediately before his own to accustom his eyes to the lights and the background. Where these are bad, he should play with extra care, keeping well on balance, giving his opponent as little chance as possible to dictate the play, and avoiding risky shots.

LARGE HALLS

Any draughts noticed should be checked when shuttle-testing and knocking-up. Accordingly, extra care must be taken in hitting to the lines and in leaving shuttles.

The sound of impact of racquet on shuttle is not as crisp as in a small hall and, because of greater air resistance, the shuttle will fly more slowly. The player should not feel his timing is wrong and be tempted to over-hit; rather he should smash a little less from deep in court.

'Landmarks', such as girders and lights, should be noted where they give a guide to leaving the shuttle.

LOW HALLS

The player should not allow himself to be put out of his normal rhythm where girders necessitate more 'lets' than usual. Drops should be taken earlier and returned if possible as net shots; smashes will tend to be less steep. Play generally will have to be faster, flatter and more accurate.

ANALYSIS OF OPPONENT

The programme should be studied and a list made of probable opponents. When these have been met before, memory should recall strengths and weaknesses; when they are unknown, their match play should be watched at every opportunity.

Such analysis should first be done by the coach, then elicited by his questions, and finally by the joint effort of coach and student. Generally it is best to sit behind or at the side of a player when studying his stroke production; opposite, when studying

142

tactics. Strengths to be avoided should be noted just as much as weaknesses to be attacked.

The student should be taught to ask himself these questions. What is his opponent's physique? Is he left- or right-handed? Is he a slow or a fast mover? Does he play an attacking or a defensive game? Is he equally sound on both forehand and backhand? Does he serve and receive equally well from both courts? Is he consistent both in length and in rallying? If he uses deception, does he betray himself in any way? Has he both determination and concentration or does he falter when losing, or even when winning comfortably? Has he the stamina to last a long game?

In particular he should notice what shots are played under pressure; whether a weakness is so well protected as to leave a gap; and whether certain favourite shots are constantly played from certain parts of the court.

To do this efficiently, the student will have to watch one player at a time; perhaps even to watch only the feet or the swing of that one player. He must learn that at times the flight of the shuttle should be ignored. Use of the chart on page 98 will facilitate such a critical appraisal, and a constantly revised record book give it permanent worth.

WARMING UP

MENTAL

This is just as important as a physical warming up. The player, having studied his opponent, mentally rehearses his tactics and works out what variations and counter-tactics he will use to deal with as many contingencies as he can reasonably foresee.

PHYSICAL

The following exercises will:

1. By dilating blood vessels, ease the cardio-vascular task.
2. By making haemoglobin denser, facilitate transmission of oxygen.
3. Change food more rapidly to energy.
4. Speed up nerve messages.
5. Increase muscle endurance and elasticity, so helping prevent pulled muscles.
6. Enable player to relax.

The exercises should be done, even in a warm changing room, after gentle massage, and in a track-suit, for some 5-15 minutes.

143

They should be performed with a relaxed and easy rhythm at gradually increasing speeds.

1. Double arm circling (feet astride).
2. Trunk twisting (feet astride: arms forward at shoulder height).
3. Skip jumping (feet together: slight bend of knees, ankles and hips on landing).
4. Knee hugging (on alternate legs).
5. Straight leg swinging (sideways to, and supported by, wall).

Such physical exercises may appear out of context in a chapter headed 'Mental Approach'. They are, however, included because they are an important phase of pre-match preparation.

OVERCOMING NERVES

Emotion kept within bounds helps the whole cardio-vascular system and quickens reflexes. Yet with it must go relaxation or early mistakes will be caused by tension of antagonistic muscles. Symptoms of over-anxiety are 'butterflies', frequent visits to the lavatory, restlessness, unusual loquacity, clammy sweating and muscular tautness. The main causes and remedies of these are as follows.

FEAR OF LOSING

If the student is the poorer player, he has little to lose and much to gain. If he is the better player, he should remember:

1. In strokes, tactics, fitness and equipment, he is fully prepared.
2. Most good players play true to form 85% of the time, above themselves 10%, below 5%.
3. It is rare for the poorer player to play above himself just when the better player is off form.
4. One loss is not irreparable disaster.

FEAR OF MAKING A FOOL OF ONESELF

Most good players are extremely generous to the weaker player. Even the 'killer' is mercifully quick and does not indulge in 'death by a thousand (deceptive) cuts'.

PRESSURE FROM OUTSIDE SOURCES

Sound newspaper criticism may be accepted but the more extravagant build-ups should be completely ignored. Over-zealous parents may have to be diplomatically curbed, asked to

144

keep in the background, or even, on occasions, to absent themselves. The coach himself, while setting his sights high, must not be over-demanding.

SUPERSTITION

Whilst the providential black cat may be tacitly accepted, the ladder and the hearse must be logically reduced to pagan irrationality.

Much good can be done by a coach in these last minutes before a game. One player will thrive on a final mental rehearsal; another will need complete distraction: to change out of sight of his opponent, to be jollied along with a fund of good jokes. If none of this works, the physical activity of the knock-up and warm-up may well do so.

STRATEGY AND ATTITUDE ON COURT

CONCENTRATION

Once the player is on court, he must concentrate *100%* on the game. This can best be achieved by :

1. Complete preparation as previously outlined.

2. Keeping the eyes focused within the court so avoiding outside distractions.

3. Watching the very base of the shuttle and trying to follow every inch of its flight from racquet to racquet.

4. Oddly enough, forcing the feet into alert, agile movement during rallies.

5. A measured pace and deep breathing between rallies. Delays caused by an opponent should be welcomed as a time for a reappraisal of tactics or as a sign of his lack of fitness, or dealt with by a polite request to player or umpire.

6. Seeing the opponent only as a striker of the shuttle and not as an inimical or unsporting personality or as a creature of annoying mannerisms.

7. Abjuring racquet-throwing, playing to the gallery and shouting.

8. Accepting official decisions, no matter how wayward, in the knowledge that they generally balance and that nothing is gained by throwing away further points in sheer pique.

9. Realizing that a preponderance of applause will naturally be for the 'local lad'.

The coach should actually train his player to play ever longer,

145

error-free rallies under simulated distractions. (The first point of a recent world-class table-tennis game was still undecided after 15 minutes!)

CONFIDENCE AND DETERMINATION

Confidence is basically the offspring of Preparation out of Concentration. The good player never becomes over-confident; the weaker player must go on court feeling that there is at least a possibility of victory and that giant-killers do exist outside *Grimm's Tales*.

Hand in hand goes determination. From the very outset, it decides to reach every shot and to score at least double-figures. It refuses to falter at an early setback, bad conditions or worse decisions, ill-luck, or an exhausted body. It regards 2-12 down in the third set as a challenge, a 'good game to win'. Determination abhors the idea of defeat until the very last stroke is played.

Confidence and determination are vital qualities which the coach must deliberately foster.

SHUTTLE TESTING

The player should learn to test ample shuttles before a game in accordance with Law 4. This will prevent irritating delays. He should remember too that the speed of shuttles may occasionally vary even when the shuttles come from the same tube. They may also vary from the first set to the third as a hall warms up, or even within a few points if they lose shape. Shuttles hit out lose points that can ill be spared. It is not bad practice, therefore, to use several shuttles of slightly different speeds in a practice game.

THE KNOCK-UP

This is not a polite formality. The player, with a crisp shuttle of correct speed, should, in a bare three minutes, do his utmost to:

1. Finally accustom himself to hall conditions.
2. Make his concentration 100%.
3. Play all shots (including serves and net shots) needed for the particular type of game he is about to play.
4. Find length, touch and accuracy.
5. Be moving fluently.
6. If knocking with his opponent, probe for weaknesses and observe strengths.

If a concentrated routine is worked out and adopted by

146

partners, they will start the first rally as well prepared mentally, physically and technically as possible. As a result they should win those first vital points instead of squandering them prodigally.

UNDERSTANDING WITH PARTNER

A cheerful understanding with one's partner, worth several points, is not achieved without some thought.

In the early days, a pre-match council of war is essential. The partners must decide: who is taking shots down the middle (low on the backhand: high on the forehand) and the majority of half-court shots; that they will call 'Mine!', 'Yours!' decisively when there is any doubt as to who will play a shot, as well as calling 'Yes!' and 'No!' early and commandingly during rallies to help each other in judging shots near the lines; sometimes to whisper intended placement of a service; which opponent to attack and the general placement of smashes, drops, clears and lobs so that the other partner is the better able to anticipate the likely return.

If A is playing badly, B's black looks, muttered asides, eyes rolling to heaven and racquet-dropping will only make him play worse. If even 'Hard luck!' or 'Good try!' sounds fulsome praise, a sympathetic grin will work wonders. If this is unavailing, two courses are still open. First, B must spot one or two of A's main errors, then quietly and succinctly offer advice. Secondly, if the rot has really set in, B must adjust his tactics. In men's and ladies', lobs and high serves should be so placed that the straight smash is to B. If B is at the net, he must drop back a little either to intercept more half-court shots or even low lobs directed to A's backhand corner. If he is at the back, B must smash for outright winners or to force a return to himself. In mixed, fast cross-courting and fast drops by the man may take the pressure off the lady.

A limited amount of agreed poaching may help doubly in that the opponents switch their play to an apparent gap which B nevertheless can still cover, while offering himself as bait.

A, for his part, must not go right into his shell and leave too much to his partner. Between rallies, he should breathe deeply and relax, trying not to show his inward concern. He must play a little more safely and try to find out the basic cause of his errors. (Poor footwork? Not watching the shuttle? Snatching? Overhitting? No follow-through? Lack of concentration?). He must try and have the confidence that he can and will play better.

When in the lead, the player must not relax. A few points carelessly thrown away by lack of concentration or by fancy shots played for the benefit of the spectators may restore a discomfited opponent's morale. A crushing defeat gives some opponents an inferiority complex which may give the winner a considerable advantage in any future encounter. Similarly, even slight physical relaxation is an equally false economy.

The winner should not ease up, particularly at the end of the first set, for the loser will make still greater efforts and probably change his tactics: the finely balanced pendulum can so easily swing the other way. Winning tactics may well be persevered with but they must never be overplayed or continued blindly against altered tactics.

The losing player should decide whether it is his strokes or his tactics that are at fault. If the former respond to more care and concentration, the latter need not necessarily be changed. If they do not, then he must evolve new tactics that are not so dependent on them. If his tactics are at fault he must obviously vary them but he should not chop and change to such an extent that they are not given a fair chance to work.

PLAYING THE PERCENTAGES

This valuable maxim is not always clearly understood. It means simply that in matches only those shots or tactics should be used which produce more winners than losers. In this context, mid-rally shots should be ignored unless they obviously bring about the subsequent winner or loser (i.e. the drop which forces a weak lob or the smash that is poked up to the net player could be counted as winners; the short clear that puts the opposition on top, and not the impossible attempt to return the resultant smash, counts as a loser).

Weak strokes or tactics revealed by such intelligent self-analysis clearly must not be entirely discarded. They must be rectified by thoughtful and intensive practice on club nights to put the player back in the winning percentages.

CRUCIAL POINTS

Theoretically every point is crucial. Some players concentrate on trying to win each rally in turn. 'I must win this point,' they urge themselves. 'I'll think about the next when I get to it.'

Many, however, cannot play with such monolithic concentration. For them, some points are more crucial than others. Such players seek to gain an early lead of three or four points. This achieved, they set their sights on being first to score eight. Next they seek to reach thirteen first so that if mischance befalls they still have a balance of five on which to draw. Steady play, without relaxation or over-confidence, coupled with an urge for a quick win, carries them over those last two elusive points.

Others, without retreating deep into a defensive shell, play carefully when their opponents are serving. They keep tape- and line-hugging shots and adventurous sorties for rallies begun on their own service. Still others regard a point lost as three points to be won : one to regain the service; one to restore the balance; and one to regain the lead.

THOUGHT DURING GAME

Too many players are just muscular automata. The mind must work as energetically throughout a long game as does the body. The successful player, almost subconsciously, after each stroke thinks of likely returns and answering shots. He uses the intervals between rallies to learn the lesson of the last one. Too critical analysis of his own stroking errors may upset his grooved reflex action or give rise to muscular tension. And after the game, a constructive, not funereal, post-mortem should be undertaken : thus, even defeat plays its part in future success.

15

COACHING ADVANCED PLAYERS

Coaching of this kind is very exacting. The ideal coach for such work should not only have the qualities previously mentioned but also have played good class county badminton. He will still play well, be fit, and be forward-looking rather than a traditionalist. Without abdicating his position, he will be prepared to discuss, experiment and share ideas rather than be too didactic.

Players seeking his help will already be fairly sound in tactics and technique. It is his difficult task to make good, better – and better, best. He must, therefore, ensure that his students attain the following standards.

GROOVED STROKE PRODUCTION

This will probably have to be brushed up from three points of view. First, all strokes, through full use of wrist and timing rather than brute strength, must be fluently powerful to conserve vital energy. Second, strokes adequate in minor badminton must be improved to hold their own even in top-class play when the pressure is really on (e.g. low serve, return of smash, backhand clear and smash). Third, they must be sufficiently grooved to withstand fatigue as well as pressure.

ACCURACY AND CONSISTENCY

The unobtrusive hallmarks of a good player are accuracy and consistency. Consistency gives nothing away even in the longest rally. Accuracy of length of drop and clear, of placement of smash, of net-hugging serves and net shots, forces an opponent into error. This is a double-edged weapon indeed.

To achieve these cardinal virtues several points must be borne

150

in mind and practised. Footwork should be good enough to allow the player to be static for a fraction of a second as he actually strikes the shuttle. The eye must not only follow the shuttle's flight intently but also be kept down for a fraction of a second after impact. As the stroke is played, the grip should be firm but relaxed; on delicate shots, good breathing should allow the breath to be held at impact. All flourishes in stroke production should be cut out because they uselessly increase the possibility of error. In the forward swing and follow-through, good balance will enable the body to lean into the shot to add control and to help keep the racquet face square to the shuttle as long as possible. Wrist action should be controlled to prevent 'snatching'.

For accuracy of placement, the racquet head must be aimed at the target as long as possible. For playing the shuttle close to the tape, 'touch' from a relaxed but firm finger-grip is essential. To give nothing away, the player must exercise ABSOLUTE CARE AND CONCENTRATION. The following practices will be found helpful (Fig. 40).

CLEARING RALLIES
(a) Players leave any shuttle not apparently falling within line marked 18 inches inside base line; (b) players leave any shuttles not dropping between two side lines or similarly marked lines running the length of the court.

DROP AND LOB RALLIES
Players leave any shuttle not dropping within 4ft of net or 18 inches of base line respectively.

PATTERN SERVING
One-foot square targets are placed in the four corners of a doubles service court. Player serves to these to any pattern, e.g. (a) low to centre; (b) flick to side line; (c) drive to centre; (d) high to side line, etc.

SMASHING
(a) From static position to target set for steepness; (b) to same target but stroke played while on the move: 12 shuttles are fed in quick succession.

DRIVES AND PUSHES
Player v two feeders; the latter leave all shots not falling between tram lines.

151

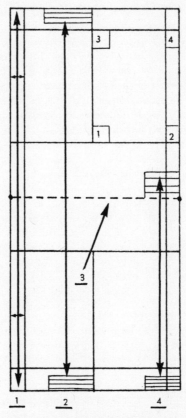

Fig. 40. Advanced consistency exercises: (1) Clears kept between tram lines, into 'boxes'. (2) Clears to be dropping on to shaded areas. (3) Ten consecutive serves into boxes in any order using high, drive, flick and low serves. (4) Slow drops and lobs to be falling on to shaded areas. (1), (2) and (4) twenty times without error.

CONSISTENCY SINGLE

Normal single but rallies kept going as long as possible while reasonably aggressive game is still played.

CONSISTENCY DOUBLES

Any player making an unforced error is replaced by a fifth player; first player displaced replaces next player to make an unforced error. Players count largest number of consecutive rallies for which they stayed on court.

152

A bonus point is allotted to whichever side wins a rally with the shuttle landing between the sidelines.

Any drop, clear or lob not going to fall between front service line and net and the two back service lines respectively are left, to count as a point lost. All smashes not falling between singles side line and line marked 18 inches inside it and parallel to it can be similarly left. Fig. 37.

DECEPTION

This is an essential quality. As it does not come naturally to all players, it must be taught. By it, opponents are worried, slowed down, or so wrong-footed as to leave an opening or be forced to make a weak return.

Since these shots involve a last split-second turn, speeding up, or slowing of the racquet face in relation to the shuttle, the margin of error is increased. They should, therefore, be played mainly when the striker is unhurried, well placed, in control; occasionally, in desperation, they may be used as a last resort. A variety of deceptive shots should be learnt but never over-played. They must be mixed in with a good proportion of straightforward or hard-hit shots which must never be sacrificed for over-much deception.

Groups of strokes must be played with a similar action: an exaggerated backswing gives the game away as obviously as does a shortened one. The grip is relaxed until impact, when it must be firm, as must the follow-through.

SIMILARITY OF SHOTS PLAYED WITH THE SAME BASIC ACTION
(a) Overhead: clear, drop, smash; (b) side-arm: drop, push, drive; (c) underarm: net shot, lob.

A plays all shots in one of the above groups to B and C who feed return shots and look for dissimilarity of action.

DEFLECTION SHOTS
A plays overarm or underarm shots, turning wrist in last foot before impact. Just before this the racquet face may have been (a) square to shuttle's line of flight; or (b) angled to right or left (before it is swiftly re-angled to make the actual shot in the other direction).

B and C feed and seek to spot intended line of flight.

153

Slightly more specialized shots in this category are: (a) round-the-head drop played from deep in left court, either straight or cross-court; (b) from same position player hits hard across the shuttle to make it drop near net in opponents' left court; (c) sliced drop – shuttle hit hard and definitely cut so deceiving by change of speed as well as of direction.

HOLDING SHOTS
A plays groups of shots as in the first practice while B and C feed and spot. In each case, the wrist is kept cocked back until the last possible second before impact so that the striker holds the threat of either hitting gently with little or no wrist action or of hitting hard with strong wrist action.

DOUBLE MOTION SHOTS
A, playing a slow-moving shuttle (e.g. in return of serve, lob, or push shot), feigns 'shot' in one direction before impact and then actually plays the shot in the other direction. B again feeds and spots.

SHOTS PLAYED IN WRONG CONTEXT
In a single, A and B both occasionally: (a) smash from the base line; (b) drop from the back doubles service line; (c) smash, not into the obvious gap, but to the side from which his opponent has just moved to cover that gap.

In other words, they play the illogical and therefore unexpected shot.

TRICK SHOTS
These should be played very sparingly indeed, in direct proportion to their success and the player's skill. Remember, too, that over-use robs them of surprise.

(a) In returning low serve on backhand, A shapes to play return cross-court, but at last second turns his hand down and round in a reverse curve to hit the shuttle in the opposite direction either as a net shot or a lob.

(b) When playing a cross-court net shot from the forehand side line, A turns his palm outwards and plays the shot with the reverse side of the racquet face. The flight of the shuttle is not altered but B is sometimes deceived by the unusual wrist action.

(c) In the right court, A shapes, a little obviously, to serve low to opposite right-hand front corner; just before impact he turns wrist to right to drive shuttle up B's backhand.

(d) A, playing an underarm net shot or drop shot, sways his body in the direction opposite to that in which he actually hits the shuttle.

PLAYING UNDER PRESSURE

Accuracy and consistency are comparatively easily achieved when the shuttle is fed slowly to the player. Now the coach must devise exercises so that the student can play his strokes equally well: (a) when the shuttle is just behind him; (b) when he has to take the shuttle at full stretch near the floor; (c) when moving fast; (d) when he is tired. (See PRESSURE TRAINING, page 132).

SPEED

Speed of thought, racquet and movement is the very essence of badminton. Unless the coach can instil this into his students they will never become first-class players (Plates 10, 15, 16 and 28).

Speed of movement is based on fitness, agility and mobility, perception and reaction, stance and movement, anticipation and analysis. All these facets of speeds must be studied and practised (see Chapter 6, pages 48–52, and Chapter 13).

STRATEGY AND TACTICS

The would-be county player must give considerable thought both to his broad strategy and his particular tactics.

TYPES OF TACTICAL GAME

He must realize that he should be able to ring the changes on five different types of game to find which his opponents like least:

(a) Power: every possible shot is hit hard, attacked.

(b) Speed: by speed of foot and eye, every shuttle is met early.

(c) Consistency: by accuracy, consistency, patience, and perhaps deception, the opponents' resistance is slowly but steadily eroded.

(d) Defensive: the shuttle is unashamedly lifted to thrust the onus of attack (where the hall is lofty or the shuttle slow) on to the opponents.

(e) Tactical: a persistent hammering at weaknesses or at just one of the opponents.

155

These may be played at as fast or slow a tempo between rallies as is consistent with sportsmanship. Which is adopted depends on the physique and temperament of both player and partner, as well as of opponents.

The player should stick to his own type of game as long as he can but must know how to counter such strategy when adopted by his opponents. In general, he should counter :

(a) Power : by keeping the shuttle low and rallies long to await the almost inevitable mistakes and perhaps weariness.

(b) Speed : by deception and a slowing of tempo.

(c) Consistency : by quick variations of general tactics.

(d) Defence : by controlled pinpointed aggression or by refusing to be drawn and, in turn, lofting the shuttle to the base line.

GENERAL TACTICAL CONSIDERATIONS
Within the general framework decided on as above, the advanced player must think about, practise by conditioned games, and employ all the tactical considerations listed on pages 99–100.

He must also realize that :

(a) What has succeeded in a lower grade of badminton may well have to be abandoned in top-class play.

(b) That height must be used both to gain and to seize time as well as to test an opponent's timing of vertically falling shuttles.

(c) That unusual and effective tactics should never be overplayed but rather kept for crucial points.

(d) That he fully understands the pros and cons of cross-courting.

PRO	CON
Enables attack to be switched to weaker opponent or gap.	Shuttle travels a greater distance and therefore more slowly.
Ensures full use of width of court. Makes return more difficult as shuttle is travelling across both line of vision and body.	Opponents have longer in which to see and move to the shuttle. Opens the angles and so forces player to cover more ground.
Provides essential variety of placement.	Unless played wisely, can be intercepted.

WIDE RANGE OF STROKES

The player must add to his armoury the following more unusual

156

strokes: (a) round-the-head smash; (b) backhand smash; (c) cut smash; (d) backhand low and flick serves; (e) round-the-back defence; (f) brush shot; (g) stab net shot; (h) stop net shot; (i) backhand lob or underhand drop shot from the back of the court with back to net; (j) round-arm, whipped clear or smash. The more of these shots he can play, the better he is equipped and the better able to cope with such shots in others.

FITNESS

If speed is the life blood of badminton, fitness is its very muscle and sinew. All depends on it. It is essential, therefore, that a schedule of training be worked out and slavishly followed.

ANALYSIS OF OPPONENTS' STROKES AND TACTICS

From both on and off court the student must learn to analyse opponents' weaknesses and strengths. It is a great advantage if he is able to spot these in the first eight points or so and thereafter to make capital out of them. The tables on pages 98–100 will help to this end. Conversely, he must quickly realize and remedy his own tactical errors and shortcomings.

TEMPERAMENT

The student must understand that his own temperament is the catalyst without which all his other qualities will never really be set ablaze. He must love and enjoy the game wholeheartedly. Burning ambition must make him realize that the top of the ladder is the only worthwhile goal. He must be a perfectionist capable of taking infinite pains. In his actual play, determination, aggression, a desire to win as many and lose as few points as possible, and a real sense of urgency must predominate. In practice, he must be dedicated to break through the boredom and pain of long months of routines and training to achieve peak physical condition. Equally important is a mental fitness that dissects opponents' play and gives rise to unswerving concentration.

He must be venturesome and imaginative enough to experiment – but not to excess. He should have that emotional stability, on and off court, that grows out of a basic inner security. Above all, he must be a good competitor who rises to a crowd, a crisis and the moment. These are the qualities that make a champion.

157

TEN GOLDEN RULES

I am indebted for this amalgam of their ideas to those great Kent and England players whom I have been fortunate enough to know so well, Ray Sharp, Paul and Sue Whetnall, Margaret Allen, Ursula Smith and Warwick Shute, and to that enthusiastic administrator, Herbert Scheele ('Mr Badminton'). These are the essence of top-class badminton. Each has been dealt with fully in these pages. Practise them indefatigably.

1. Ability to play a wide range of shots – under pressure, too.
2. Infinite variation of returns and tactics.
3. Ability quickly to analyse opponents' weaknesses.
4. Imperturbability in face of bad decisions and conditions.
5. Unflagging concentration and care to avoid unforced errors.
6. Absolute fitness and speed of foot, hand and mind.
7. Determination and guts.
8. Eagerness to watch good play critically and to learn from others.
9. Playing frequently at top-class club, league, county and tournament standard.
10. Preparation and Practice; Patience, Perspicacity and Persistence.

How admirably did *The Times* lawn tennis correspondent hammer home these points when, in describing the Rumanian Tiriac's play in the Davis Cup v Great Britain, he wrote, 'His fundamental strategy was to watch the ball every second it was in play; get to it; think constructively; and then take maximum care with the stroke itself while still going for winners and putting the ball in the most awkward places. He seldom made an error that was not forced upon him.'

16

VALUE AND ENJOYMENT
OF COACHING

Had you doubted the value of coaching, it is unlikely that you would have reached this page. However, for the sceptic, the dismal Jeremiah, the unconverted, let me point out again that few novices acquire correct techniques or tactics naturally. In supplying this knowledge, the coach is saving his student from falling into wrong methods hard to eradicate, is saving him laborious hours of trial and error, is giving him ideas that might never have crossed his mind. Nor is every student a student of psychology, physical education and diet to boot. A coach is a short cut by which his students more speedily reach greater fitness, enjoyment and ability. In mere weeks or months he is giving the distilled essence of his own years of badminton.

And the fun and enjoyment? Believe me, it's limitless; as your playing skill declines and you foresee a bleak vista of badminton senility ahead, coaching opens up new horizons. Now you must learn to think as never before and get really fit again. Here is a chance to put back into the game all that you so avidly took from it; to meet a host of new friends, both playing and administrative; to mingle with youngsters and to share their triumphs; to make the deep, lasting relationships that are essential in successful coaching; to rise to the top again, this time as a coach.

For myself, I have met hundreds of grand people and have visited dozens of interesting places. To name people would be endless and invidious, but I shall never forget happy hours at Lilleshall Hall in its superbly wooded grounds; at Inverclyde with its breathtaking view across the sail-flecked waters of the Clyde to the jagged peaks of Arran; at Crystal Palace, with its soaring cathedral-like columns and its superb Olympic pool; at Durham with its magnificent view of Castle and Cathedral on the other side of the Bede College dining table; at Loughborough with its skyscraper hostels around the base of which the wind always howls; at Lea Green, Matlock, with its fine leather-panelled lounge and pastoral setting; at Valletta, Malta, with its superb Grand Harbour; and at Kingston, Jamaica, with its marvellous back-drop of the Blue Mountains. Coaching has given me much.

ACKNOWLEDGMENTS

I would like to express my sincere thanks to:

Ray Sharp, Paul and Sue Whetnall, and, especially, Margaret Allen and Tyna Barinaga, who travelled so far to show how it really should be done;

Graham Barclay, who spent so much time and trouble in taking most of the photographs;

Peter Roper and all the boys and girls on the Lilleshall Young Players' Course, July 1969;

George Popplewell, Director of Physical Recreation at the University of Kent at Canterbury, who vetted the chapter on 'Physical Fitness' and permitted us to take photographs in the Sports Hall;

Brian Jelfs, Senior Lecturer in PE at Christ Church College of Education, who again unhesitatingly allowed me the use of his gymnasium;

Dr Peter Travers of St Luke's College, Exeter, who worked out the specialized weight-training exercises;

Ray Greenstreet of Canterbury Technical High School for Boys, who gave me much advice on the preparation of the diagrams;

Nancy Horner for her never failing help and encouragement;

My life-long secretary (who now deciphers Egyptian hiero-glyphics with ease) for typing, retyping and typing yet again.